CRICKET GROUNDS

from the air

ZAKI COOPER & DANIEL LIGHTMAN

AERIAL PHOTOGRAPHY

IAN HAY

MYRIAD

LONDON

CONTENTS

Below: one of the most beautiful cricket grounds in the world, Arundel is used by Sussex for both County Championship matches and one-day games.

First published in 2009 by Myriad Books Limited, 35 Bishopsthorpe Road, London SE26 4PA
www.myriadbooks.com

Photographs© Ian Hay/Flight Images

Text © Zaki Cooper & Daniel Lightman

Zaki Cooper & Daniel Lightman have asserted their rights under the Copyright, Designs & Patents Act 1998 to be identified as the authors of this work.

ISBN 1 84746 269 3   EAN 978 1 84746 269 5

Designed by Jerry Goldie Graphic Design

Printed in China

Photographs in the Famous Players sections supplied by David Frith, Getty Images, The Sportsphoto Agency Photographic Library, Associated Sports Photography and Daniel Lightman.

PREFACE

The wonderful aerial photographs taken by Ian Hay enable the reader to view the UK's major cricket grounds from a spectacular new perspective.

To help to bring the grounds to life, each chapter features personal recollections, provided especially for this book, of the grounds which are pictured and described. More than 100 cricketers' recollections have been obtained, from all of the ten Test-playing countries and spanning the generations from the 1930s, when Cyril Perkins played for Northamptonshire, to contemporary players. Whilst many of those who have provided their reminiscences are renowned for their cricketing feats, some are now better known for their achievements in other fields, including football (Sir Geoff Hurst), rugby ("Dusty" Hare) and the legal world (Lord Griffiths).

We are grateful to the men (and one woman!) who have generously and freely given of their time and memories to provide their recollections for this book. We would like to thank Geoffrey Boycott, a childhood hero of both of ours, for the Introduction. For the help they have given we would also like to thank Harvey Freeman, David Frith, Rakesh Jagota, Gary Newbon, Nigel Peters QC, David Relf, Vernon Smith QC, Dr Maurice Smith and Rabia Zia, as well as the counties' press offices. We are especially grateful to Benedict Bermange, the Sky Sports statistician, for patiently answering our many factual and statistical queries and for calculating the run averages for each ground. Finally, we would like to express our appreciation to our wives, Rachel and Felicia, for their patient indulgence of our cricketing passion, and to our parents Judy and John, Naomi and Gavin, for all their support.

Zaki Cooper and Daniel Lightman

Guide to information boxes

BOX 1: COUNTY RECORDS
Formed in: the date on which the county was officially established. Unless it was a founding member of the County Championship in 1890, the date on which the county was admitted to the Championship is added in brackets.
County Champions: this includes only the titles won (including shared titles) after the County Championship was officially established in 1890 (before which finishing top meant you became Champion County). In 1895 it was expanded from nine to 14 counties. Second Division titles, which have been awarded since the counties split into two divisions from the 2000 season, have not been included. When a county has not won the Championship, the best finish is listed.
Gillette/NatWest/C&G/FP: this one-day tournament has gone through various incarnations. It started as the Gillette Cup in 1963, as a 65-over-a-side competition, switched to 60 overs-a-side in 1964 and became the NatWest Trophy in 1981, the C&G Trophy in 2001 and is now the Friends Provident Trophy. The format became 50 overs-a-side in 1999.
Benson & Hedges: the 55-over one-day competition called the Benson & Hedges which was established in 1972 but came to an end in 2002.
Sunday League: this is the 40-over competition originally called the John Player League which was repackaged to become the National League in 1999 (when two Divisions were formed) and

subsequently the Pro40 in 2006.
Twenty20: the 20-overs-a-side tournament was introduced in 2003.
The leading run-scorer/wicket-taker and wicket-keeping dismissals: in first-class cricket only. In each case the name of the player is followed by the dates he played for the county and then the total number of runs/wickets/ wicket-keeping dismissals for the county is listed. 'Av' refers to the average and wicket-keeping dismissals are broken down into catches (ct) and stumpings (st).
Most capped England player: the Tests in which a player appeared while playing for the given county. The years given are those between which he represented the county.
Average first innings total in first-class matches, average runs per wicket in first-class matches, and average runs per over in limited overs matches: these figures have been calculated by Benedict Bermange by reference to all of the matches played in the 10 years between 1999 and 2008 at each county's primary ground – except for the Rose Bowl, where Hampshire have only played since 2001. The figures confirm that Taunton is the best ground in the country for batting – and the Riverside the worst.
The information in the tables and boxes is up-to-date as at 31 December 2008.

BOX 2: COUNTY GROUND FACTS
In the boxes giving information on the main ground, we have used the following guidelines:
Capacity: these figures have been difficult to obtain but in most cases the information has been provided by the counties themselves. However, the capacity of many grounds can be augmented by temporary stands.
First County Match: the first match played by the county at the ground; the date given is the first day of the match.
First Test Match: where a Test Match has been played, the first Test played there is listed; the date given is the first day of that Test.
First ODI: where a one-day international match has been played at the ground, the first such match is listed. Since England has hosted the World Cup on four occasions (in 1975, 1979 1983 and 1999, when it shared hosting responsibilities with the other home nations and the Netherlands) the match is sometimes one between countries other than England.
Record crowd: this has proved to be an extremely difficult statistic to obtain and the information given is in many cases based on best estimates given by the relevant county. The figure for the record crowd is often far higher than the official capacity as, in the old days, crowds would often be permitted to watch from the boundary edge, unrestricted by stands.

INTRODUCTION

We may not have the biggest cricket grounds in the world but we certainly have some of the most beautiful, historic and prestigious. From the world-famous Lord's and Old Trafford to the picturesque settings at the likes of Canterbury and Worcester, the UK is home to some of the finest grounds in the world.

In a 25-year career I was fortunate to play 492 first-class matches in the UK on 49 different grounds. My favourite is, unfortunately, no longer a cricket ground. It is Bramall Lane, now the home of Sheffield United Football Club.

I had a great love for Bramall Lane. I was so sad when Yorkshire stopped playing there in 1973. The turf was gorgeous – I have never seen anything like it in my life. When they closed down the ground, I bought some of the turf and planted it in my mother's garden.

The pavilion was old, as befitting the fact that Yorkshire cricket started in Sheffield, in 1855. Bramall Lane was Yorkshire County Cricket Club's headquarters before it moved to Leeds.

We had some colourful characters in Sheffield. One was 18-stone Yorkshire Annie, who had a deep and very loud voice. She used to sit right by the opposition dressing room balcony and would irritate Yorkshire's opponents with her shouts of "Go on York-shire, wheel them in and wheel them out!", or her urging on Fred Trueman, "Bowl them a bouncer, Freddie!" Bramall Lane was right in the centre of Sheffield, a five-

Geoffrey Boycott and rival Lancashire captain David Lloyd before the Yorkshire v Lancashire game at Bramall Lane on 4 August 1973, the last match to be played at the ground.

minute walk from the railway station. People could take a couple of hours off work in the middle of the day to catch a bit of the cricket. There is a lovely story that when the opposition was batting, they would stoke up the chimneys in the Sheffield steel mills, so that the resultant smoke would prevent the batsmen from seeing the ball clearly.

Some of my most memorable cricketing experiences took place at Bramall Lane. I scored my first century in first-class cricket there, in the Roses Match in June 1963, in front of a 20,000 crowd. It was at Bramall Lane, too, that Fred Trueman led us to a famous victory over the Australians in 1968.

Happy memories like that are what cricket is all about. The stunning aerial photographs in this book will, no doubt, evoke many warm memories in its readers. Cricketers ranging from Sir Alec Bedser, recalling the first match at The Oval after the Second World War, more than 60 years ago, to contemporary stars share their happy experiences of the grounds featured. I am pleased, too, that readers will gain some insight into the histories of the grounds and some of the leading cricketers who played there.

Impressive cricket grounds located all over Britain are proof of cricket's enduring appeal. While we have many beautiful old grounds, we have also seen a sprouting of new grounds in recent years. Redevelopment is taking place up and down the country. In particular, the main grounds in Durham, Hampshire and Glamorgan have all been developed with a view to their hosting Test Matches. This book enables us to enjoy our cricketing memories and to look forward to many great matches to be played at these fantastic venues in the future.

Geoffrey Boycott OBE

Right: Headingley Carnegie, home of Yorkshire CCC.

Devon Malcolm on the County Cricket Ground, Derby:

"I played at the old Racecourse Ground, Derby for 14 years, starting out as a 21-year-old. In April time, at the start of a cricket season, it was often the coldest and windiest place to play cricket and I loved it. Despite the weather, the pitch was good, and was not as rough or abrasive as many other grounds. As a bowler, it was still possible to extract swing after 65-70 overs. I have some very happy memories of playing at Derby and particularly remember the time I took seven wickets in a NatWest game in 1997, ironically against Northants for whom I later played. I pop back to Derby when I get the time, and the ground has been totally transformed."

DERBYSHIRE

Derbyshire CCC was formed at a meeting in the Guildhall, Derby in November 1870. The following summer the club played its first first-class match, against Lancashire at Old Trafford. While starting promisingly, it then did so poorly that in 1888 it lost its first-class status but was able to recover it six years later. Derbyshire continued to struggle, its nadir being 1920, when it lost 17 of 18 games, the other match being abandoned without a ball bowled.

From the late 1920s Derbyshire developed a strong bowling attack, led by the brothers George and Alf Pope, pace bowler Bill Copson, leg-spinner Tommy Mitchell and all-rounder Les Townsend. With support from the elegant batting of Denis Smith and Stan Worthington – the first Derbyshire player to score a Test century – in 1936 Arthur Richardson led Derbyshire to their only Championship.

After the Second World War, Derbyshire continued to have a fearsome bowling attack, led by their leading wicket-taker Les Jackson with Cliff Gladwin and, subsequently, Harold Rhodes, which was particularly effective on Derby's green wickets. While Donald Carr, who captained England in India in 1951-52, and Arnold Hamer were useful batsmen, their batting was far less formidable than their seam bowling. Nor – apart from off-spinners Edwin Smith and Geoff Miller – were they strong in the spin bowling department.

The combative South African Eddie Barlow injected not just runs, wickets and catches at short-leg but also a fighting spirit into the team, which was built on by Kim Barnett in his 13 years as captain of the side between 1983 and 1995. One-day successes

COUNTY RECORDS

Formed in 1870 (admitted to the Championship in 1895)
County Champions 1936
Gillette/NatWest/C&G/FP 1981
Benson & Hedges 1993
Sunday League 1990
Twenty20 Best – Quarter-finals 2005
Nickname of one-day team
Phantoms

Leading run-scorer Kim Barnett
(1979-98) 23,854 (av 41.12)
Leading wicket-taker Les Jackson
(1947-63) 1,670 (av 17.11)
Most wicket-keeping dismissals
Bob Taylor (1961-84) 1,304 (1,157 ct, 147 st)
Most capped England player
Bob Taylor (1961-84) – 57 Tests

COUNTY GROUND AVERAGES
First innings total in first-class matches 311
Runs per wicket in first-class matches 31.64
Runs per over in limited overs matches 4.80

included the NatWest Trophy in 1981 and the Sunday League in 1990.

However, in recent times the team has languished in the lower reaches of Division Two of the County Championship. Some hope for the future was given by a more encouraging Championship campaign in 2008, with excellent contributions from the dependable South African paceman Charl Langeveldt and the exciting left-handed Australian batsman Chris Rogers. At Edgbaston against Warwickshire Rogers made 248 not out. He ran out of partners 26 short of the 112-year-old record for the highest score for Derbyshire, George Davidson's 274 against Lancashire in 1896.

The County Cricket Ground, Derby

Since 1871 the home of Derbyshire CCC, the County Cricket Ground was for many years known as the Racecourse Ground, as it was previously located in the centre of a racecourse. After horse-racing ended in 1939, the cricket square was moved to its present location. In 1982 the county purchased a 125-year lease of the ground from Derby County Council. In July 2004 permanent floodlights were installed at the County Cricket Ground.

Although it can be bleak on a wet or windy day, owing to the lack of cover, the ground has been redeveloped, with facilities including an indoor school. In the last few years the setting sun behind the bowler's arm at the Scoreboard End has caused several day/night and Twenty20 games to be halted. This has prompted the county to rotate the square 90 degrees and to relocate the scoreboard and floodlights, and at the same time to demolish the old jockey quarters – the last remnant of the ground's past life as a racecourse.

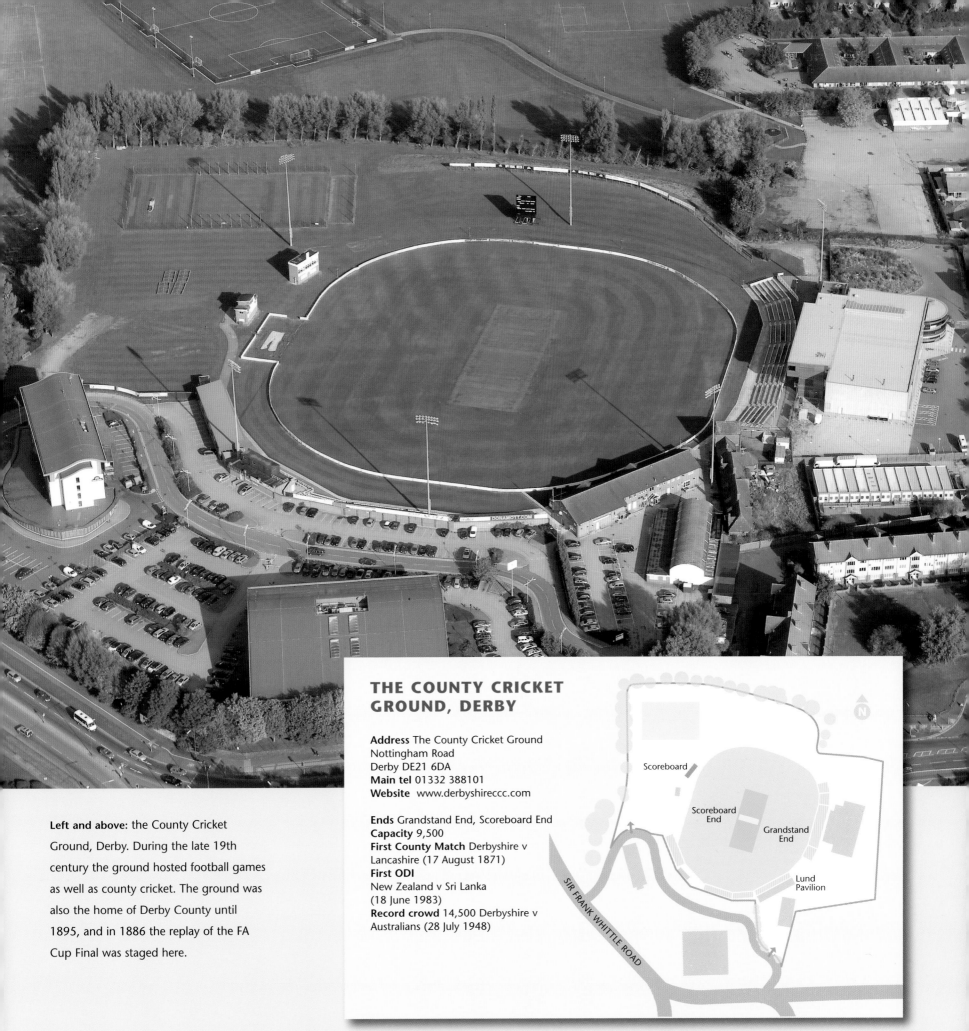

THE COUNTY CRICKET GROUND, DERBY

Address The County Cricket Ground
Nottingham Road
Derby DE21 6DA
Main tel 01332 388101
Website www.derbyshireccc.com

Ends Grandstand End, Scoreboard End
Capacity 9,500
First County Match Derbyshire v
Lancashire (17 August 1871)
First ODI
New Zealand v Sri Lanka
(18 June 1983)
Record crowd 14,500 Derbyshire v
Australians (28 July 1948)

Scoreboard

Scoreboard
End

Grandstand
End

Lund
Pavilion

SIR FRANK WHITTLE ROAD

Left and above: the County Cricket
Ground, Derby. During the late 19th
century the ground hosted football games
as well as county cricket. The ground was
also the home of Derby County until
1895, and in 1886 the replay of the FA
Cup Final was staged here.

OTHER GROUNDS

Queen's Park, Chesterfield

As its name suggests, Queen's Park lies within a park in the middle of Chesterfield. It was established in 1897 in honour of Queen Victoria's Diamond Jubilee. A beautiful tree-lined ground, with a bandstand and small pavilion, it is overlooked by the crooked spire of All Saints church.

Queen's Park quickly gained a place in cricket folklore as the very first match played there, in 1898, saw the Yorkshire opening batsmen, JT Brown (300) and John Tunnicliffe (243) put on a then world-record 554 runs for the first wicket – in just over five hours! Six years later Derbyshire won a memorable game by nine wickets, even though Percy Perrin scored 343 not out (including a world-record 68 fours) in Essex's first innings: Charles Olivierre scored 229 and 92 not out for Derbyshire, who bundled Essex out in their second innings for 97.

The home of Chesterfield CC, Queen's Park saw no county cricket between 1998 and 2005, but Derbyshire returned, following an extensive refurbishment of the ground, in 2006. Derbyshire now play 10 days' cricket at Queen's Park every year: two Championship matches, a one-day game and a Twenty20 game.

Harold Rhodes on Queen's Park:
"My favourite cricket ground is Queen's Park, Chesterfield, with its famous crooked spire, boating lake, scenic railway, beautiful gardens and, most important, the best supported ground in Derbyshire. In the mid-1950s I was granted leave from National Service to play against Yorkshire there. It was a wonderful game with Derbyshire enjoying a rare win by six runs on the final day. I took five wickets, including the last. To beat Yorkshire in those days was some achievement and a great start for my career."

FAMOUS PLAYERS

Les Jackson

Les Jackson (1921-2007) was perhaps the most feared fast bowler in county cricket in the 1950s. With a slingy action, he moved the ball at speed both ways and got the ball to lift awkwardly, inflicting bruises on many batsmen. He was also very accurate and economical. Jackson took more wickets for Derbyshire than anyone else, but was only picked for England twice – one Test in 1949, the other some 12 years later. Since he bowled well in both games, some say his non-selection was due to the selectors' snobbery towards an ex-miner. When he retired Jackson finished with a total of 1,733 wickets at the exceptionally good average of 17.36, and best figures of 9-17.

Donald Carr

Born in 1926, Donald Carr made his first-class debut in 1945, aged just 18, for England at Lord's in the Victory Test against Australia. First playing for Derbyshire in 1946, he captained Cambridge University in 1950, Derbyshire between 1955 and 1962 and England in one Test in India in 1951-52.

A graceful batsman, especially good against fast bowlers, in 1959 he scored a county record 2,292 runs for Derbyshire. Carr scored almost 20,000 runs in his career, as well as taking 328 wickets with his left-arm spin. An excellent close-in fielder, he ended up with exactly 500 catches. After he retired Carr became a cricket administrator at Lord's, where his son, John, enjoyed success playing for Middlesex.

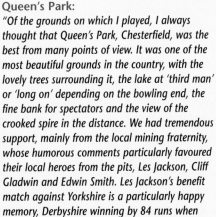

Donald Carr on Queen's Park:

"Of the grounds on which I played, I always thought that Queen's Park, Chesterfield, was the best from many points of view. It was one of the most beautiful grounds in the country, with the lovely trees surrounding it, the lake at 'third man' or 'long on' depending on the bowling end, the fine bank for spectators and the view of the crooked spire in the distance. We had tremendous support, mainly from the local mining fraternity, whose humorous comments particularly favoured their local heroes from the pits, Les Jackson, Cliff Gladwin and Edwin Smith. Les Jackson's benefit match against Yorkshire is a particularly happy memory, Derbyshire winning by 84 runs when Laurie Johnson leapt for a high catch at slip with about three minutes remaining. The humbling of Middlesex for 29 was another success, which might have been even better as they had been 13 for 9 before Bennett and Moss more than doubled the score for the last wicket. However, it was not always a success story for the home county. The Gloucestershire brothers Graveney seemed to enjoy the Chesterfield ground, Ken taking all 10 wickets in an innings one year – he helped me to a 'king pair' – while Tom made a lovely double century a year or two later."

Harold Rhodes

Harold Rhodes (born 1936) was the son of Derbyshire all-rounder AEG Rhodes (1916-1983), a leg-spinning all-rounder who took five hat-tricks and later umpired eight Test Matches. At first an off-spinner, Harold Rhodes developed into a fast bowler. He made an immediate impact in the first of his two Tests against India in 1959, taking a wicket in each of his first two overs. In the following year, however, he was no-balled for throwing. Rhodes' fight to clear his name – told in his book *The Harold Rhodes Affair* – eventually led the MCC, which had extensively investigated his bowling action, to clear him in 1968, declaring that he had a "hyper-extended arm".

By then, however, it was too late for Rhodes' Test career to resume. In 1965 Rhodes topped the English bowling averages with 119 wickets at the remarkably low average of 11.04.

Bob Taylor

Bob Taylor (born 1941) is regarded as one of the greatest of all wicket-keepers. None has held more catches than his total of 1,473 or had more dismissals than his 1,649. Taylor played for Derbyshire for 24 seasons, between 1961 and 1984, and was county captain in 1975 and part of 1976.

Denied a place in the Test team for many years by Alan Knott's superior batting skills, Knott's ban after joining World Series Cricket allowed Taylor to become an England regular. He played 57 Tests, highlights being his then-record 10 catches in the Jubilee Test against India in 1979-80 and his crucial seventh wicket partnership of 135 with Derbyshire colleague Geoff Miller in the deciding Test against Australia at Adelaide in 1978-79. Agonisingly, Taylor was dismissed for 97. Fortunately, in 1981, aged 40, he scored his one and only century – exactly 100 for Derbyshire against Yorkshire.

Bob Taylor on Queen's Park:

"Queen's Park, Chesterfield is one of the prettiest of grounds, with its crooked church spire. It is also a family-friendly ground, which appealed to me more than anything.

Two games spring to mind. One was the game between Derbyshire and the 1965 South African touring team. We batted quite well and I think the South Africans were caught cold. In the end we won the match by seven wickets. We were the only team to beat the tourists that year – England lost the Test series 1-0. For our endeavours, we won 12 bottles of South African sherry, one for each team member and one for the 12th man. The other was the semi-final of the Gillette Cup in 1969 against Sussex. We struggled to 136 all out. The strong Sussex batting line-up were confident of victory – they needed to score at little more than two runs per over. But we bowled them out for just 49, Peter Eyre taking 6-18 – a tremendous performance."

Devon Malcolm

Born in 1963, Devon Malcolm was for a time England's fastest bowler. Although erratic and sometimes expensive, he could be explosive. He single-handedly won the Oval Test of 1994, destroying the South African batting. His second innings figures of 9-57 were (and remain) the best by an English fast bowler since 1895-96. In 40 Tests, Malcolm took 128 wickets (av 37.09). He would have played more Tests but for his poor fielding and batting – he averaged just 6.05 with the bat – and if he had not fallen out with the then England manager, Ray Illingworth. Malcolm played for Derbyshire between 1984 and 1997, after which, following two years with Northamptonshire, he ended his career with Leicestershire. In his last season he took his 1,000th first-class wicket.

DURHAM

Located in the north-east of England, a region renowned for its sporting passion, Durham have made their mark on English cricket, hosting their first Test Match at the Riverside in 2003 and producing home-grown talents such as Paul Collingwood and Steve Harmison for the national team. The youngest county made history in the 2008 season by winning the Championship for the first time. This was a significant landmark, just 16 years after the granting of first-class status in 1992, for a club which had been founded 110 years earlier.

Durham's history goes back to the late 19th century. The county won its first match against Northumberland in June 1882, played at Ashbrooke Cricket Ground, Sunderland. It soon established itself as a formidable force in Minor Counties cricket where it first played in 1899, winning five championships by 1930. It then endured a 46-year barren spell (including the ignominy of finishing bottom in 1953), before regaining its dominant status from 1976 onwards. Indeed the club achieved the record for the longest unbeaten spell in Minor Counties cricket, spanning 65 matches between 1976 and 1982 (the championship was won in three of those seasons) and in 1984 won the Minor Counties title for the ninth time.

In 1973 Durham became the first Minor Counties side to defeat a first-class county when they toppled Yorkshire in the Gillette Cup. In 1985 they beat Derbyshire in the NatWest Trophy, to become the first minor county to defeat a first-class team twice.

Geoff Cook on the Riverside:
"Having been at Durham since the beginning, it's been great to see the Riverside take shape. The setting of the ground with the backdrop of Lumley Castle is really impressive and to play at home is always a special occasion for the team. The development work scheduled to take place over the next few years will make it one of the best grounds in the country. I also think other teams who play here enjoy the ground, especially in front of the North-East crowds."

COUNTY RECORDS

Formed in 1882 (admitted to the Championship in 1992)
County Champions 2008
Gillette/NatWest/C&G/FP 2007
Benson & Hedges Best – Quarter-finals 1998, 2000, 2001
Sunday League Best – 8th (Div One) 2002, 2006
Twenty20 Best – Semi-finals 2008
Nickname of one-day team Dynamos

Leading run-scorer Jon Lewis (1997-2006) 7,854 (av 31.41)
Leading wicket-taker Simon Brown (1992-2002) 518 (av 28.30)
Most wicket-keeping dismissals Phil Mustard (2002-) 289 (277 ct, 12 st)
Most capped England player Steve Harmison (1996-) 58 Tests

COUNTY GROUND AVERAGES
Average first innings total in first-class matches 302
Average runs per wicket in first-class matches 28.46
Average runs per over in limited overs matches 4.58

Throughout these years, the North-East had a reputation for producing talented players, like Bob Willis and Peter Willey, who had to move south to advance their careers.

In 1989 the board of Durham Cricket Club applied for first-class status, which was granted in December 1991, on condition that a new ground suitable for hosting Test Matches would be built. Durham thereby became the first new county admitted to the Championship since Glamorgan 70 years earlier.

Durham played in the County Championship for the first time in the 1992 season. Their very first match was against Leicestershire at the Racecourse Ground in Durham. Until the construction of the new ground at the Riverside, opened in 1995, Durham played at a variety of grounds in the

county. During the 1992 season, for instance, home venues included Gateshead, Jesmond, Darlington and Stockton-on-Tees.

Durham took a while to adjust to the higher standards of first-class cricket, finishing in the bottom three of the Championship in each of their first six seasons. However, with the help of experienced professionals including Ian Botham, David

THE RIVERSIDE, CHESTER-LE-STREET

Address The Riverside Ground, Riverside Complex, Ropery Lane, Chester-le-Street
Co Durham DH3 3QR
Main tel 0191 387 1717
Website www.durhamccc.co.uk

Ends Finchale End, Lumley End
Capacity 7,000 (16,000 with temporary seating)
First County Match Durham v Warwickshire (18 May 1995)
First Test Match England v Zimbabwe (5 June 2003)
First ODI Pakistan v Scotland (20 May 1999)
Record crowd 16,000 England v Australia ODI (23 June 2005)

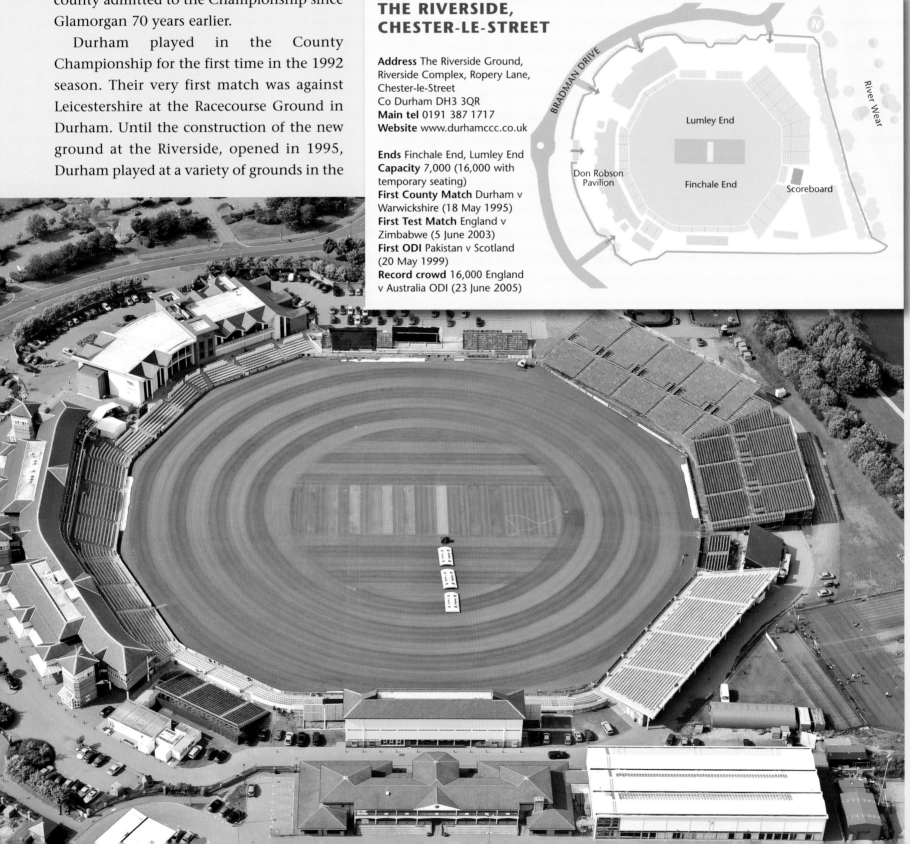

Graveney, Dean Jones and Simon Hughes, and a growing cohort of gifted younger players, the county eventually made much progress. This improvement culminated in the successful 2007 season, when Durham won their first major title, the Friends Provident Trophy, and just missed out on the Championship to Sussex by the slender margin of 4.5 points. Yet further success soon followed, with the historic Championship victory in the 2008 season, when Nottinghamshire were overhauled on the final day, as a result of Durham's victory over Kent at Canterbury; the *coup de grace* was administered by Harmison, who took the final two Kent wickets in two balls – the latter his 60th Championship wicket of the season – to seal his county's first Championship title.

The Riverside, Chester-le-Street

In 1993, a year after being granted first-class status, Durham received permission to build their own ground at the Riverside and to develop 6.3 hectares of land overlooked by Lumley Castle. It was envisaged that the ground would be able to play host to international cricket, bringing Test Matches to the sports-obsessed North-East for the first time. The project was funded by the club, with the support of Durham County Council and Chester-le-Street District Council. Set in beautiful surroundings, the Riverside includes other amenities such as a public park, an athletics track and football pitches. In addition to hosting top-class sport, it is also a music venue.

The new ground was opened in 1995 and Durham played their first match there against Warwickshire. The stadium was built in three distinct phases between 1995 and 1997, with facilities for players and spectators being added in stages.

In October 1996, the Queen officially opened the Don Robson Pavilion, named after a local politician who had been instrumental in bringing first-class cricket to the North-East. There are a total of six permanent stands on the western and southern ends of the ground,

while the northern and eastern sides have tiered tip-up seats.

The Riverside did not have to wait long for its first taste of international cricket: in 1999 it hosted two World Cup matches. The following year an England one-day international was held against the West Indies. England's Test Match against Zimbabwe in June 2003 marked the historic occasion of the first Test at the Riverside. In the process it became the first new Test ground in England since 1902 when Bramall Lane hosted its only, and Edgbaston its first, Test. Further Tests have been held at the Riverside against Bangladesh in 2005 and the West Indies in 2007 and 2009.

OTHER GROUNDS

Feetham's Cricket Ground, Darlington *above*

Durham played their first Minor Counties match at Darlington in 1895 against Cheshire. The ground had been opened in 1866 after Darlington moved from their nearby Park Street ground. The pavilion was built in 1903 and the spacious grounds can accommodate 20 pitches. After Durham achieved first-class status, the local council invested £20,000 towards improving facilities. The ground now has a capacity of approximately 5,000 and has become a popular second home for Durham's matches since hosting its first county match against Somerset in 1992.

Grangefield Road, Stockton-on-Tees *right*

Durham have used the Grangefield Road ground for matches since 1947. Established in 1891, after Stockton Cricket Club moved there, the ground has a capacity of approximately 4,000.

FAMOUS PLAYERS

Clive Leach

Clive Leach (born 1934) was an all-rounder who played 39 first-class matches for Warwickshire between 1955 and 1958, before joining the then Minor County Durham in 1960, for whom he played until 1964. Following a 30-year career in television, including a spell as chief executive of Tyne Tees Television, in 2004 he returned to Durham as Chairman. In that role he built a successful business model and led the county to unprecedented success on the field, including a first Championship trophy in 2008.

Clive Leach on the Riverside:

"I played for Durham as a professional when it was a Minor County side, soon after my exit from first-class cricket with Warwickshire. We played at lovely grounds, including Ashbrooke in Sunderland, Durham, Redcar and my home ground of Bishop Auckland where I was the club professional, and all of us dreamt of Durham acquiring first-class status and a first-class ground to go with it. To be now the Chairman, following five years of hard work and commitment by so many people, of the Champion County and a genuine Test Match ground, probably the loveliest in the country, is a dream come true. Credit must be given to those who had the foresight some 20 years ago to select the Riverside site and start the journey of aspiration now being substantially fulfilled. But now the consolidation must take place and we must go on from here."

Geoff Cook

If anyone can be described as the heart and soul of Durham, it is Geoff Cook (born 1951) who joined the county in 1991 as captain. The following year he was appointed Director of Cricket for Durham's first season in first-class cricket. In the ensuing years he was responsible for the county's academy, which produced a clutch of high-calibre players. He took over as Durham coach from Martyn Moxon for the 2007 season, and guided the team to its first Championship in 2008, which he describes as his "proudest achievement". As a player, Cook was a capable opening batsman, playing mainly for Northamptonshire, whom he captained between 1981 and 1990. In total he scored 23,277 runs from 460 first-class matches.

A purple patch of form, combined with the rebel tour of South Africa, gave him an opening to the England Test side, for whom he played seven times in the early 1980s.

David Graveney

David Graveney (born in 1953) is best known these days as a senior cricket official, having served as Chairman of the England Test Selectors between 1997 and 2008 and for several years as Chief Executive of the Professional Cricketers Association. Born into a distinguished cricketing family – his father Ken captained Gloucestershire, as did his famous uncle Tom – he played county cricket for 22 years, most of it at Gloucestershire from 1972 to 1990 (skippering the team for most of the 1980s) and at Somerset for one season; he ended up captaining Durham between 1992 and 1994, the county's first three seasons in the County Championship. In 457 first-class matches, he took 981 wickets with his left-arm spin bowling. He was also a useful lower-order batsman.

David Graveney on the Riverside:

"I dug the first bit of earth at the Riverside with a JCB. I remember seeing the site when it had no cricket ground. And now there is a fantastic ground, which epitomises what Durham is all about. As I finished my Durham career in 1994, I never

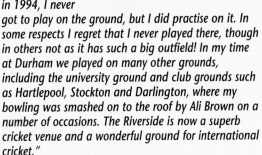

got to play on the ground, but I did practise on it. In some respects I regret that I never played there, though in others not as it has such a big outfield! In my time at Durham we played on many other grounds, including the university ground and club grounds such as Hartlepool, Stockton and Darlington, where my bowling was smashed on to the roof by Ali Brown on a number of occasions. The Riverside is now a superb cricket venue and a wonderful ground for international cricket."

Steve Harmison

Steve Harmison is a local boy who was born in Ashington, Northumberland, in 1978. He made his Durham debut in 1996. A fast bowler with a fearsome reputation when on form, he made his England debut in 2002. He shot to prominence for his devastating spell of bowling against the West

Indies at Sabina Park in March 2004, finishing with the remarkable figures of 7-12. While his international career has been up and down, another highlight was the role he played in England recapturing the Ashes in the summer of 2005, the first time the national side had beaten the Aussies in a series since 1987. He has made a major contribution to Durham's recent successes. In the 2008 season, he took a total of 65 first-class wickets in 14 matches (finishing the second highest wicket-taker in the country) at an average of 22.86.

Graham Onions

Born in Gateshead in 1982, Onions made his debut for Durham in the 2004 season. The medium-fast bowler and useful lower-order batsman impressed in the 2006 season (with 50 Championship wickets) at the end of which he was selected for England's squad for the ICC Champions Trophy. After an injury-affected 2008, strong early-season form in 2009 led to Onions making his Test debut at Lord's: remarkably in the West Indians' first innings he took 5-38, including four wickets in seven balls.

Graham Onions on the Riverside:

"To step out into the middle of such a magnificent pitch sends shivers down your spine. The ground is in a great setting and the ground staff work hard to prepare quality pitches. As a local lad it is always special walking out to the middle and, hopefully, getting wickets! I was lucky enough to be playing in the match against Hampshire at the Riverside in July 2007 when Ottis Gibson took all 10 wickets in an innings. He just kept bowling from one end, picking up wicket after wicket. You could sense the excitement building around the ground as he approached the magic 10. It was a special moment when he picked up the tenth wicket. He wheeled away in jubilation and you could feel from the fans and players their excitement at this special achievement. It is something which may never happen again at the Riverside or in my career so I will always remember it."

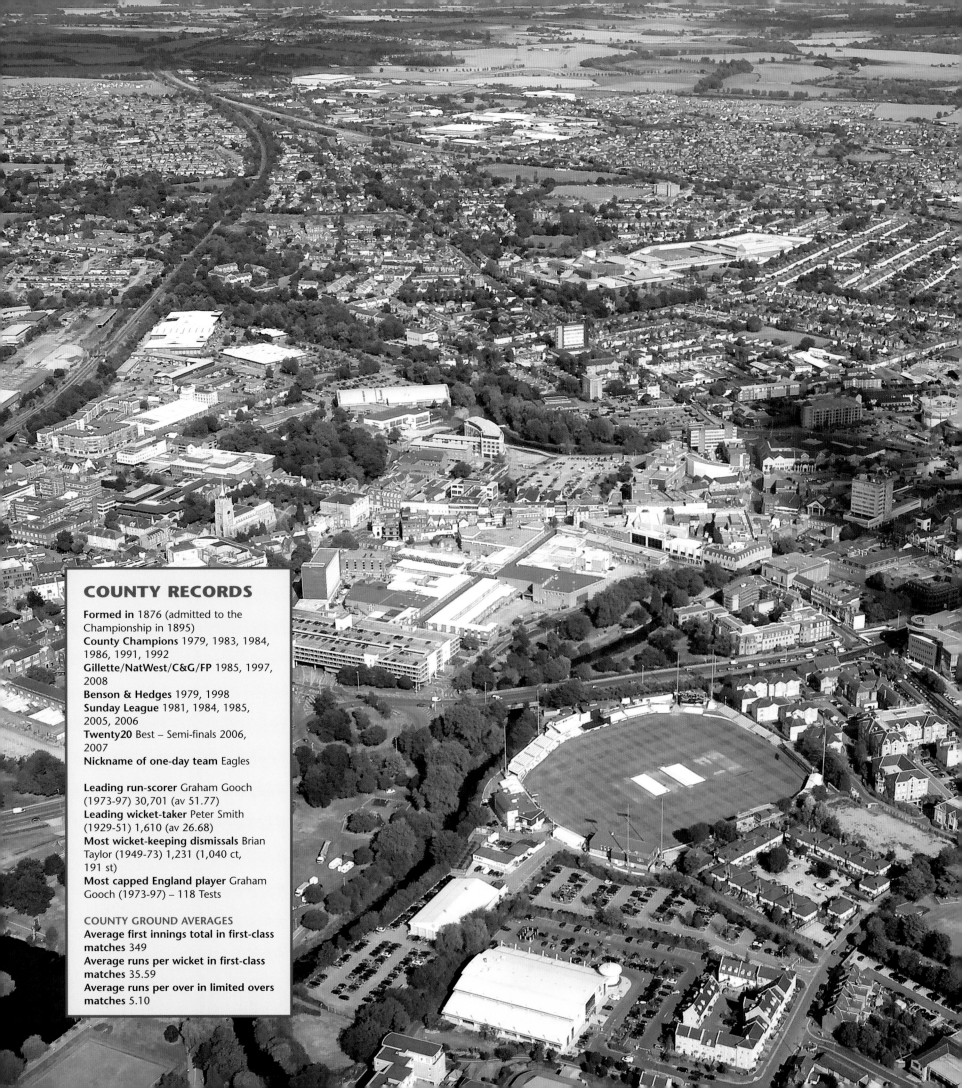

COUNTY RECORDS

Formed in 1876 (admitted to the Championship in 1895)
County Champions 1979, 1983, 1984, 1986, 1991, 1992
Gillette/NatWest/C&G/FP 1985, 1997, 2008
Benson & Hedges 1979, 1998
Sunday League 1981, 1984, 1985, 2005, 2006
Twenty20 Best – Semi-finals 2006, 2007
Nickname of one-day team Eagles

Leading run-scorer Graham Gooch (1973-97) 30,701 (av 51.77)
Leading wicket-taker Peter Smith (1929-51) 1,610 (av 26.68)
Most wicket-keeping dismissals Brian Taylor (1949-73) 1,231 (1,040 ct, 191 st)
Most capped England player Graham Gooch (1973-97) – 118 Tests

COUNTY GROUND AVERAGES
Average first innings total in first-class matches 349
Average runs per wicket in first-class matches 35.59
Average runs per over in limited overs matches 5.10

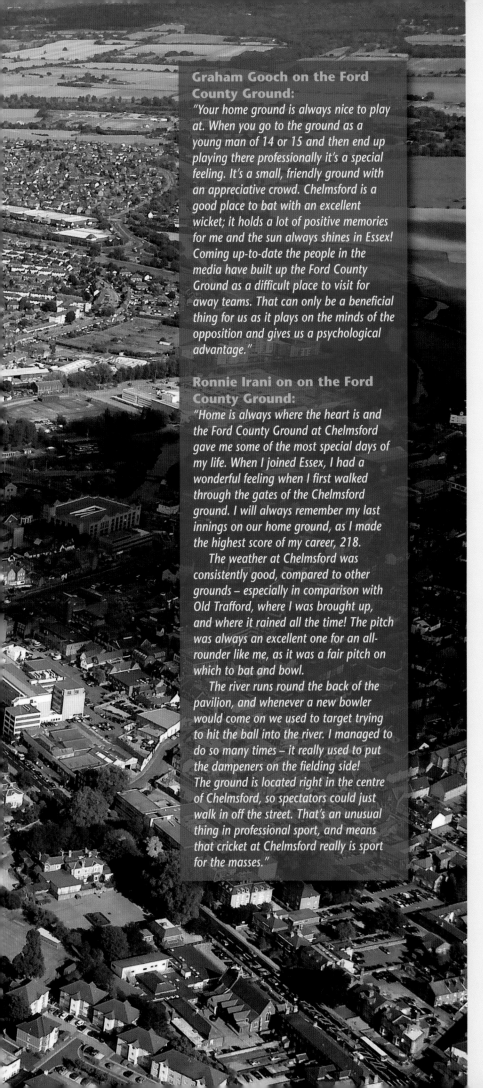

ESSEX

Essex were formed in 1876 but had to wait for more than a century before enjoying the most successful spell in their history. They won their first County Championship in 1979 and five more between then and 1992, together with an array of one-day titles. Led by inspirational captains Keith Fletcher and Graham Gooch, Essex enjoyed a golden age in their cricketing history.

Essex County Cricket Club was established on 14 January 1876, and played its opening first-class match against Leicestershire at Leyton in May 1894. In 1895 it was admitted to the Championship and finished ninth under the leadership of HG Owen; the team soon made huge strides, vying for the title for much of the 1897 season and eventually finishing third.

The county began to produce some talented players who made their mark. PA Perrin scored nearly 30,000 runs in first-class cricket, including 66 centuries, but perhaps owing to his weak fielding was never picked for England. Under the captaincy of JWHT Douglas, who led the team from 1911 to 1928, performances steadily improved. The leg-spin bowler Peter Smith made his debut in 1929 and was a key part of the side in the 1930s, as was batsman Jack O'Connor, who scored over 1,000 runs in each of 15 consecutive seasons in the run-up to the Second World War.

Following the sale of their main ground at Leyton in 1933, Essex moved between nine different venues over successive decades, until Chelmsford became their permanent headquarters in 1967. This travelling to different grounds established their reputation as the nomads of English cricket. The post-War era produced such distinguished cricketers as Doug Insole, who captained the team from 1950 and was its most reliable batsman, and all-rounder Trevor Bailey, a key player for England in the 1950s (as well as Insole's successor as captain). Yet the county found consistency elusive, and suffered the ignominy of picking up the Championship wooden spoon in 1950. There was also the occasion when the Essex bowling attack was savaged by the touring Australians, who scored 721 runs in one day's play in 1948.

But the 1970s, and in particular Fletcher assuming the captaincy in 1974, marked the beginning of a renaissance. For the next 20 years, the county's devoted following were treated to many titles. The disappointment of a second place finish in 1978, largely due to bad luck with the weather, was followed by Essex's first Championship title in 1979. The triumph was resounding, as 13 matches were won in the season, and the county also picked up the Benson and Hedges Cup. Further trophies were won during the 1980s and 1990s in both the long and the short versions of the game, and a number of Essex favourites went on to play for England, including captains Graham Gooch and Nasser Hussain.

The Ford County Ground, Chelmsford

Essex first staged a Championship match at Chelmsford in 1926, against Somerset. The ground, situated near the river Can, was used periodically by Essex with the permission of Chelmsford Cricket Club, who rented it from a trust.

However, it was not until 1967 that Chelmsford became the permanent home of Essex cricket, when the county established its headquarters there. This had been made possible by a generous gesture from Warwickshire CCC supporters' association, in the form of a £15,000 interest-free loan in 1964.

The pavilion was completed in 1970 and other stands have been added since. In 2002 floodlights were installed. For a time the ground was used as an emergency helicopter landing area for a nearby hospital. At the ground, Essex have enjoyed the most successful spell in their history, becoming a force to be reckoned with in the English county game. Graham Gooch scored 8,710 runs at Chelmsford at an average of 54.77, including his highest score for the county, 275 made against Kent in 1988. The county

Doug Insole on the Ford County Ground:
"Probably my most vivid memory of the Chelmsford ground is of Essex bowling out Surrey for 14 in 14 overs in 1983 - the lowest team total in first-class cricket since 1907. Neil Foster (4-10) and Norbert Phillip (6-4) shared the wickets on a placid pitch on which, in their second innings, Surrey scored 185 for 3."

currently have plans to redevelop the Chelmsford ground, which would involve a complete overhaul. It will increase the capacity to 8,000 and is intended to be completed by the 2011 season.

THE FORD COUNTY GROUND, CHELMSFORD

Address The Ford County Ground New Writtle Street, Chelmsford Essex CM2 0PG
Main tel 01245 252420
Website www.essexcricket.org.uk

Ends River End, Hayes Close End
Capacity 8,000
First County Match Essex v Oxford University (20 June 1925)
First ODI Australia v India (20 June 1983)
Record crowd 7,300 – Twenty20, Essex v Kent (20 June 2003)

Pavilion

River Can

Hayes Close End

River End

Score board

A1060

OTHER GROUNDS

Castle Park, Colchester *below*

The picturesque Castle Park Ground, situated near the river Colne, is the home of Colchester and East Essex Cricket Club (founded in 1862). The ground was opened in 1908 and six years later Essex played their first game there. They returned after the First World War but because of the frequency of flooding and poor drainage transferred to the nearby Garrison Cricket Ground between 1966 and 1974. History was made at Castle Park in 1938 when Kent batsman Arthur Fagg became the first – and only – batsman to hit a double century in each innings. Nowadays the ground often attracts crowds of 5,000 to watch the Essex team in action.

Southend

Essex have used three grounds in Southend for first-class cricket: Chalkwell Park, Southchurch Park and Garon Park. Chalkwell Park became a regular home for Essex matches after the county left their Leyton ground in 1933. They continued to play there until 1976, and the ground is still used by Westcliff-on-Sea Cricket Club. Nearby Southchurch Park was used by Essex to host matches in Southend Cricket Week from 1906; it famously hosted the match against Don Bradman's Australians in May 1948, watched by a huge crowd of 16,000, when the Australians scored 721 runs in a day and Bradman 187 in 125 minutes.

In 1989 the pitch at Southchurch used for a match against Yorkshire was reported to the authorities as unfit for purpose, which led to a penalty of 25 points, damaging Essex's aspirations to win the Championship (Worcestershire finished the season six points above them).

Garon Park is a modern purpose-built cricket ground, first used by Essex in 2004. The ground was built on the edge of attractive parkland just north of Southend and is the venue for the Essex Summer Cricket Festival, which features one-day and County Championship games. The festival normally takes place in late July and early August.

FAMOUS PLAYERS

Johnny Douglas

JWHT Douglas (1882-1930), whose slow batting once prompted a wag to claim that his initials stood for "Johnny Won't Hit Today", was captain of Essex between 1911 and 1928, and the most dominant personality at the club during his career. A powerfully-built and brave competitor – he won the Olympic middle-weight boxing title in 1908 – Douglas recovered from the trauma of being bowled by George Hirst for 0 in both innings of his debut for Essex in 1901 to score more than 24,000 runs and take almost 1,900 wickets in his career. In a match against Derbyshire in May 1921 he followed up his highest innings – 210 not out – with his best bowling figures: 9-47. As England captain, he won the Ashes in Australia in 1911-12, but later led England to defeats in seven successive Ashes Tests, including all five Tests on the 1920-21 tour. Douglas drowned at sea trying to save his father after the ship they were on collided with another boat in thick fog.

Trevor Bailey

Born in 1923, Trevor Bailey played for Essex for more than two decades from 1946 to 1967, and he played a total of 682 first-class matches. One of the few players who have scored more than 20,000 runs and taken more than 2,000 wickets, he was an often obdurate batsman, who once batted 458 minutes for 68 runs in an Ashes Test. He scored one double century – 205 – for Essex. With his fast-medium swing bowling he performed the rare feat of taking all 10 wickets in an innings, for Essex against Lancashire at Clacton in 1949. In a Test Match in the West Indies in 1953-54 he destroyed the powerful West Indies batting line-up, taking 7-34. He performed the double of 1,000 runs and 100 wickets in a season on eight occasions. In 1959, he was the last man to score 2,000 runs and take 100 wickets in a season. Bailey played 61 Tests for England between 1949 and 1959, with his batting average of 29.74 slightly higher than his bowling average of 29.21. However, figures do not give the full story: he made vital contributions to the Ashes triumphs of 1953 and 1954-55. After his Test career ended, Bailey captained Essex between 1961 and 1966. He later became well-known as a voice of cricket on *Test Match Special*, where he was nicknamed "The Boil".

Trevor Bailey on Chalkwell Park, Southend:
"My favourite ground is my home ground, Chalkwell Park, Westcliff-on-Sea. I was born and brought up in Westcliff. My family home was a five-minute walk from the Chalkwell Park ground – we were so close that I could change at home. I played club cricket there for Westcliff in the 1930s and again in the 1970s, with my son, after I finished playing for Essex. I still sometimes go on a Saturday afternoon to watch Westcliff playing there. Chalkwell Park is a little ground. The facilities were limited; there were no nets there suitable for county cricket to practise before the game. Runs would come quickly. Sixes were comparatively easy to hit, and the ball was quite often hit into the road by the ground. But it was also a lively wicket, a good wicket for the quicker bowlers to bowl on."

Doug Insole

After captaining the Cambridge University team in 1949, Doug Insole (born 1926) went on to captain Essex throughout the 1950s. Through his leadership and consistent batting, the team's performances started to improve, though a Championship title proved elusive. Insole was also a useful bowler and – as befitted a talented amateur footballer – an exceptional slip fielder; he even kept wicket on occasion. By the time he played his last match in 1963, he had amassed over 25,000 first-class runs and 54 hundreds (one of them a match-saving 110 not out in six hours against South Africa), and played nine Tests for England. After retirement, he was an England selector for nine years and chairman of the Test and County Cricket Board. In 2006, at the age of 80, he became MCC President.

Graham Gooch

Born in 1953, Graham Gooch was a key member of the successful county teams which won six Championships from 1979 onwards and a number of one-day titles. A commanding opening batsman, he broke many county batting records in his career which spanned from 1973 to 1997. For instance, the 2,559 runs he amassed in the 1984 season and the 30,701 runs and 94 first-class centuries he scored for Essex are all county records. His Test debut was famous for bagging a pair against the Australians in 1975, but he returned as a regular to the Test arena three years later and it was after his appointment as England captain in 1988 that he really flourished as a batsman. He scored 333 and 123 against India at Lords in 1990 (becoming the only batsman to score both a triple century and a century in a Test Match) and the following year a memorable 154 not out against the West Indies at Headingley in the most trying of circumstances to help England to a famous victory. By the time he retired from Test cricket in 1995, he had scored 8,900 runs – more than any other Englishman – in 118 matches.

Sir Geoff Hurst

Famed for his footballing exploits, as the man who scored a hat-trick in the 1966 World Cup Final, many people don't realise that Geoff Hurst (born 1941) also played first-class cricket. Being a West Ham player, naturally his county was Essex. His sole first-class game was in 1962 against Lancashire at Liverpool (he scored 0 not out and 0 and took a catch). In three seasons between 1962 and 1964 he played 23 Second XI Championship matches. His record as a batsman for the Essex second team was 797 runs in 41 innings (av 20.43) with four fifties. Fortunately for English football, he gave up county cricket and concentrated on the "winter game", and his achievements are an indelible part of footballing folklore.

Ronnie Irani

A popular figure on the county circuit, the career of Ronnie Irani (born 1971) thrived after he left Lancashire for Essex in 1994. Some eye-catching all-round performances led to his Test debut in 1996. In total he only played three Tests, but he was a more regular feature of the England one-day side, playing 31 one-day internationals. Irani became Essex captain in 2000 and in addition to these responsibilities, became Essex player-coach in 2005. By that time, he had been forced to stop bowling owing to injury problems, which eventually led to his premature retirement in 2007. He went out with a bang though; his last three innings at Chelmsford yielded scores of 144, 28 not out and 218. Irani is one of the very few cricketers who in their first-class careers averaged more than 40 with the bat and less than 30 with the ball.

GLAMORGAN

Glamorgan CCC was founded in 1888. It competed in the Minor County Championship until, in 1921, it successfully applied to join the County Championship – the last county to do so until Durham 70 years later. It started encouragingly, winning its first match, against Sussex, but thereafter its results were so poor that *Wisden* expressed the view that its entry into first-class cricket had not been justified by results. Of its three professional players, two were 47 years old! The rest of the team was made up of a number of mediocre amateurs.

In 1930 Maurice Turnbull, who the previous winter had become the first Glamorgan player to be capped by England, became Glamorgan captain. He also became the club secretary. Turnbull held both positions throughout the 1930s, and as well as improving the club's financial position, he helped to set up a settled team with a core of useful professional players. In 1937, Glamorgan won 13 out of 30 games, and finished seventh in the Championship, off-spinner JC Clay taking 176 wickets (av 17.36) for the county, a record which still stands.

In 1948, under the inspiring captaincy of all-rounder Wilfred Wooller, Glamorgan won the Championship, largely because of their excellent fielding, especially in the leg-trap, where 120 catches were held that season. Clay, who had first appeared for Glamorgan in their debut season of 1921, played a key role on the spin-friendly August pitches. In the next few years Glamorgan were unable to repeat that success, partly because other counties got used to their leg-side theory, although their team included England players all-rounder Allan Watkins,

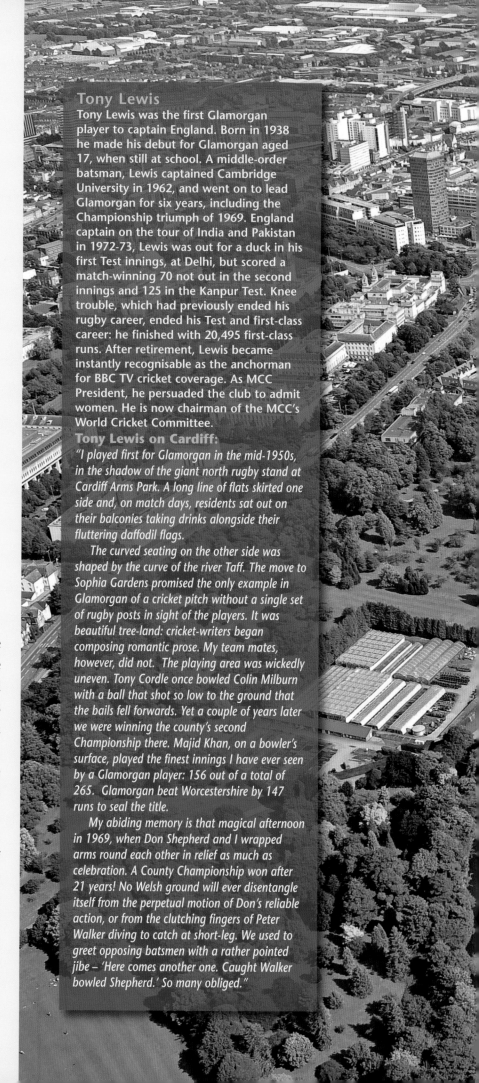

Tony Lewis
Tony Lewis was the first Glamorgan player to captain England. Born in 1938 he made his debut for Glamorgan aged 17, when still at school. A middle-order batsman, Lewis captained Cambridge University in 1962, and went on to lead Glamorgan for six years, including the Championship triumph of 1969. England captain on the tour of India and Pakistan in 1972-73, Lewis was out for a duck in his first Test innings, at Delhi, but scored a match-winning 70 not out in the second innings and 125 in the Kanpur Test. Knee trouble, which had previously ended his rugby career, ended his Test and first-class career: he finished with 20,495 first-class runs. After retirement, Lewis became instantly recognisable as the anchorman for BBC TV cricket coverage. As MCC President, he persuaded the club to admit women. He is now chairman of the MCC's World Cricket Committee.

Tony Lewis on Cardiff:
"I played first for Glamorgan in the mid-1950s, in the shadow of the giant north rugby stand at Cardiff Arms Park. A long line of flats skirted one side and, on match days, residents sat out on their balconies taking drinks alongside their fluttering daffodil flags.

The curved seating on the other side was shaped by the curve of the river Taff. The move to Sophia Gardens promised the only example in Glamorgan of a cricket pitch without a single set of rugby posts in sight of the players. It was beautiful tree-land: cricket-writers began composing romantic prose. My team mates, however, did not. The playing area was wickedly uneven. Tony Cordle once bowled Colin Milburn with a ball that shot so low to the ground that the bails fell forwards. Yet a couple of years later we were winning the county's second Championship there. Majid Khan, on a bowler's surface, played the finest innings I have ever seen by a Glamorgan player: 156 out of a total of 265. Glamorgan beat Worcestershire by 147 runs to seal the title.

My abiding memory is that magical afternoon in 1969, when Don Shepherd and I wrapped arms round each other in relief as much as celebration. A County Championship won after 21 years! No Welsh ground will ever disentangle itself from the perpetual motion of Don's reliable action, or from the clutching fingers of Peter Walker diving to catch at short-leg. We used to greet opposing batsmen with a rather pointed jibe – 'Here comes another one. Caught Walker bowled Shepherd.' So many obliged."

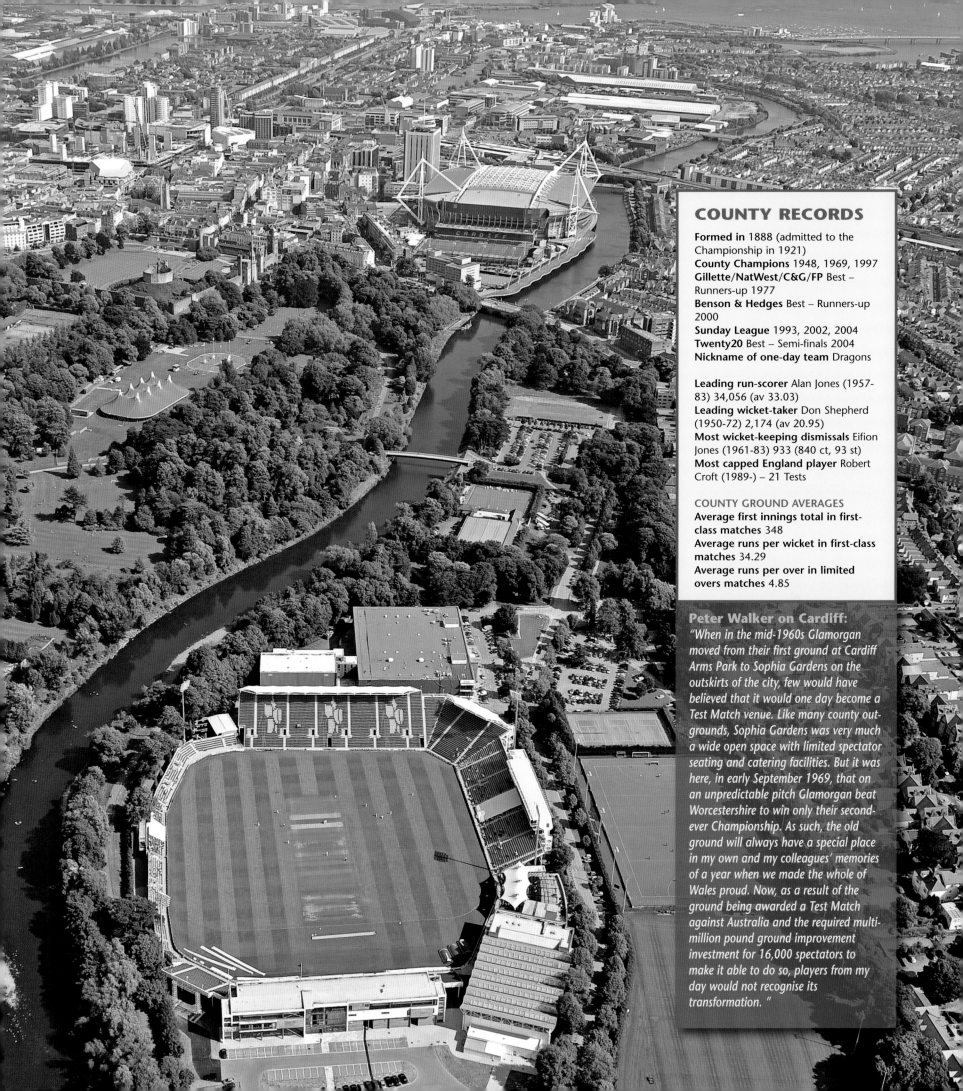

COUNTY RECORDS

Formed in 1888 (admitted to the Championship in 1921)
County Champions 1948, 1969, 1997
Gillette/NatWest/C&G/FP Best – Runners-up 1977
Benson & Hedges Best – Runners-up 2000
Sunday League 1993, 2002, 2004
Twenty20 Best – Semi-finals 2004
Nickname of one-day team Dragons

Leading run-scorer Alan Jones (1957-83) 34,056 (av 33.03)
Leading wicket-taker Don Shepherd (1950-72) 2,174 (av 20.95)
Most wicket-keeping dismissals Eifion Jones (1961-83) 933 (840 ct, 93 st)
Most capped England player Robert Croft (1989-) – 21 Tests

COUNTY GROUND AVERAGES
Average first innings total in first-class matches 348
Average runs per wicket in first-class matches 34.29
Average runs per over in limited overs matches 4.85

Peter Walker on Cardiff:
"When in the mid-1960s Glamorgan moved from their first ground at Cardiff Arms Park to Sophia Gardens on the outskirts of the city, few would have believed that it would one day become a Test Match venue. Like many county out-grounds, Sophia Gardens was very much a wide open space with limited spectator seating and catering facilities. But it was here, in early September 1969, that on an unpredictable pitch Glamorgan beat Worcestershire to win only their second-ever Championship. As such, the old ground will always have a special place in my own and my colleagues' memories of a year when we made the whole of Wales proud. Now, as a result of the ground being awarded a Test Match against Australia and the required multi-million pound ground improvement investment for 16,000 spectators to make it able to do so, players from my day would not recognise its transformation."

spinner Jim McConnon and Don Shepherd, one of the best bowlers never to play Test cricket.

After finishing second in 1963, and third in both 1965 and 1968, in 1969 Glamorgan won the Championship again, under the captaincy of Tony Lewis. The first county since Lancashire in 1930 to go through the whole season undefeated, the team featured the batting of Lewis, Alan Jones and the Pakistani Majid Khan, the all-round skills of Peter Walker, and the bowling of Shepherd, Tony Cordle and Malcolm Nash.

The 1970s and 1980s were lean years for Glamorgan cricket, one of the few highlights taking place in 1977 when Alan Jones led them to the final of the Gillette Cup. The county had eight captains in less than a decade.

A revival occurred in the 1990s. Viv Richards helped Glamorgan win the Sunday League in 1993 and another destructive batsman, Matthew Maynard, led Glamorgan to their third Championship in 1997. That side, which was coached by Duncan Fletcher, also featured opening batsman Steve James, who in 2000 went on to make the first triple century for Glamorgan, and Pakistani Waqar Younis, who was renowned for his fast reverse-swinging yorkers. Sunday League triumphs followed in 2002 and 2004, but following relegation in 2005 Glamorgan have languished in Division Two of the County Championship.

The SWALEC Stadium, Cardiff

Glamorgan first played at Sophia Gardens in 1967, after the cricket ground at Cardiff Arms Park had been subsumed within a new national rugby stadium. The ground is to the north of the ornamental gardens named after Sophia, the wife of the second Marquess of Bute, who laid out recreational grounds for the use of the residents of Cardiff. In 1969 Sophia Gardens hosted the emotional match in which Glamorgan defeated Worcestershire to win the Championship.

Some notable batting feats have taken place at the ground. For example, in 1990 Jimmy Cook of Somerset scored 313 not out, and in 1993 Viv Richards and Adrian Dale shared an unbroken fourth wicket partnership of 425 against Middlesex. While this remains the highest-ever partnership for the club for any wicket, Glamorgan went on to lose the match.

For the first time in its history Glamorgan had its own permanent ground when, in 1995, the club acquired a 125-year

lease of Sophia Gardens. It has since developed the ground as its headquarters, with a National Cricket Centre, which was opened in 1999. Sophia Gardens has hosted a number of one-day internationals, including floodlit day/night matches. After 18 months' substantial refurbishment and rebuilding work, which transformed the ground's capacity from 6,500 to 16,000, a new stadium was opened in May 2008. Renamed the SWALEC Stadium under a 10-year, £1.5m sponsorship deal with an energy supplier, the second phase of the building works is due to be completed in time for the first Test Match to be held in Wales, the Ashes opener in July 2009.

Matthew Maynard

Born in 1966, Matthew Maynard was a prolific and fast-scoring batsman for Glamorgan from 1985 to 2004, playing four Tests for England. He finished with the record for the most centuries for the county (54), and scored almost 25,000 runs (av 42.53). As captain of Glamorgan between 1995-2000, he led the club to the Championship in 1997.

Matthew Maynard on Cardiff:

"I made my debut at Cardiff in 1985 and until my last game there for Glamorgan in 2004 always enjoyed playing there. Probably my most cherished memory was when I scored my 53rd hundred for my county, against Leicestershire in 2004. It broke the record for the highest number of centuries for Glamorgan, previously held by Hugh Morris and Alan Jones. When it happened the 12th man brought me a small glass of whisky out to the middle, but dropped some of it on his way! With all the improvements it's a lovely ground and hosting a Test Match there will be a significant landmark in Welsh cricketing history."

THE SWALEC STADIUM, CARDIFF

Address The SWALEC Stadium, Cardiff CF11 9XR
Main tel 0871 282 3401
Website www.glamorgancricket.com

Ends River Taff End, Cathedral Road End
Capacity 16,000
First County Match Glamorgan v Indians (24 May 1967)
First Test Match Due to be England v Australia (8 July 2009)
First ODI Australia v New Zealand (20 May 1999)
Record crowd 15,000 England v South Africa (2 September 2008 – only 3 overs' play were possible owing to rain!)

River Taff

Scoreboard

River Taff End

Pavilion

Cathedral Road End

SOPHIA GARDENS

OTHER GROUNDS

St Helen's Ground, Swansea *above*

Cricket has been played at St Helen's since 1873, and Glamorgan have played there since 1921. Named after a convent dedicated to Saint Helen, it is the home of the Swansea Cricket and Football Club and hosted international rugby matches from 1882 until 1954. There are 45 steps from the players' pavilion down to the field of play, which is dominated by two 140ft-high floodlit pylons, as the ground is built on a reclaimed sandbank. In places the soil is very thin.

Many famous matches have been played at St Helen's. They include Glamorgan's victory over the Australians in 1964, which was watched by a record 50,000 spectators. There have been some famous feats of six-hitting, with batsmen taking advantage of the relatively short straight boundaries. Malcolm Nash bore the brunt of this more than anyone else, being hit by Gary Sobers for six sixes in one over in 1968 and for 34 runs in an over by Frank Hayes nine years later. In 1976 Clive Lloyd hit a double century in two hours for the West Indians, equalling Gilbert Jessop's record. Lloyd would have broken Jessop's record had the scorers not failed to stop the clock for a drink's break in the middle of his innings.

The Rhos Ground, Rhos-on-Sea *right*

The home of Colwyn Bay Cricket Club since 1924, the Rhos Road ground was used by Denbighshire for its home Minor Counties fixtures. With the backing of Wilfred Wooller, who was brought up in Rhos-on-Sea and whose father had helped to found the ground, between 1966 and 1971 Glamorgan played an annual fixture there. In the game against Leicestershire in 1969, Glamorgan paceman Tony Cordle took 9-49, both the best figures of his career and the ground record. Financial pressures led to the end of the Colwyn Bay festival in 1974, but Glamorgan returned to Rhos-on-Sea for the Championship match against neighbouring Lancashire between 1990 and 1995. In 2000 Steve James made 309 not out against Sussex, sharing a county-record opening stand of 374 with the Australian Matthew Elliott.

FAMOUS PLAYERS

Don Shepherd

Born in 1927, Don Shepherd was the mainstay of Glamorgan's bowling attack for more than 20 years. Making his debut in 1950 as a fast-medium bowler, in 1955 he switched to off-cutters. The following season he took 177 wickets. On his retirement, in 1972, he was Glamorgan's leading wicket-taker. His final haul of 2,218 wickets is the most by any man who never played Test cricket. His accuracy and economy are illustrated by the fact that on average he conceded just two runs an over and one-third of the overs he bowled in his career were maidens. An attacking tail-end batsman, Shepherd did not stick around at the wicket: in all cricketing history only two rabbits have exceeded the 149 ducks he made in his career, but Shepherd scored 51 against the 1961 Australians in just 15 minutes and 11 scoring shots – six sixes, three fours, a two and a single. Three of the sixes were hit off Richie Benaud, who stated: "That was the greatest bit of sustained hitting that I have seen in my life."

Peter Walker

Born in Bristol in 1936, Peter Walker had, in 1961, perhaps the best all-round season ever: his middle-order batting yielded 1,347 runs, a mixture of medium-paced seam and slow spin reaped 101 wickets, and as a brave and brilliant short-leg he took 73 catches. In the previous season he had enjoyed some success in three Tests for England against South Africa – the country in which he spent his childhood. Playing for Glamorgan between 1956 and 1972, Walker was a key member of the Championship-winning side of 1969. After retiring with 17,650 runs, 834 wickets and 697 catches, Walker became a well-known commentator. He later served as the chief executive of the Cricket Board of Wales, and is now president of Glamorgan CCC.

Paul Sheahan

Paul Sheahan (born 1946) was a graceful Australian batsman and perhaps the finest cover-point fielder of his generation. He played for Victoria, for whom at the age of 20 he scored 202 against South Australia. He went on to play 31 Tests, scoring 1,594 runs (av 33.91), but retired at his peak at the age of 27 to pursue a career in education. He is now the Headmaster of Melbourne Grammar School. He made 137 for the Australians in their game against Glamorgan at St Helen's in 1972.

Paul Sheahan on St Helen's Cricket Ground:

"The fixture between Australia and Glamorgan was always seen by the locals as the 'sixth Test', so there is 'ginger' in every one of these contests. I recall playing on this unpretentious but historic ground in 1972 particularly, when Australia, following a defeat at the hands of the Welsh in 1964 and 1968 anticipated a hat-trick... and that is just what they achieved! Whether this milestone was due to impeccable planning and peerless execution of the strategy or, what was more likely, overwhelming hospitality, I'll leave for others to judge. The inescapable fact is that, if a national loss can ever be justified for the vanquished, it was justified in 1972! The singing of the crowd after that third straight win, which included the Welsh national anthem and other songs that stirred the soul, sounded as if it were emanating straight from the valleys – it was an enormous privilege to see and hear how a tiny nation galvanises itself with pride in circumstances like that, and the memory will stay with me forever. The fact that I also happened to make one of my few centuries at St Helen's helps, of course!"

Athar Ali Khan

Born in Dacca in 1962, Athar Ali Khan was an all-rounder who played 19 one-day internationals for Bangladesh between 1988 and 1998, scoring 532 runs (av 29.55). He made his highest score, 82, against Pakistan in 1997. He is currently a Bangladesh national selector and a cricket commentator.

Athar Ali Khan on Cardiff:

"Growing up as a keen student of history, I always wondered how it was possible for David to beat Goliath. The Mohammed Ali vs Sonny Liston fight (the first one!) gave us the answer in more than one way. Representing Bangladesh as an opening batsman, I was always up against it and in most cases Goliath would triumph! In 2005, when I was touring the mother country as a member of the commentary team, I saw Bangladesh take on the might of the Australians in an ODI in Cardiff. The Aussie juggernaut was on a roll until it came across a 5ft 2in wall – a destructive wall called Mohammed Ashraful, who played the greatest ODI innings in our history. Bangladesh beat Australia and Sophia Gardens, Cardiff, became a household name in Dhaka! The Cardiff ground will go down in our folklore as the place where the greatest triumph for this young cricketing nation took place!"

COUNTY RECORDS

Formed in 1871
County Champions Best – Runners-up
in 1930, 1931, 1947, 1959, 1969 and 1986
Gillette/NatWest/C&G/FP 1973, 1999,
2000, 2003, 2004
Benson & Hedges 1977, 1999, 2000
Sunday League Best – Runners-up in 1988
Twenty20 Best – Runners-up in 2007
Nickname of one-day team Gladiators

Leading run-scorer Walter Hammond
(1920-51) 33,664 (av 57.05)
Leading wicket-taker Charlie Parker (1903-
35) 3,170 (av 19.43)
Most wicket-keeping dismissals "Jack"
Russell (1981-2004) 1,054 (950 ct, 104 st)
Most capped England player
Walter Hammond (1920-51) – 85 Tests

COUNTY GROUND AVERAGES
**Average first innings total in first-class
matches** 321
**Average runs per wicket in first-class
matches** 32.75
**Average runs per over in limited overs
matches** 4.75

GLOUCESTERSHIRE

Whilst the first recorded cricket match in Gloucestershire took place as early as 1729, the present club was founded in 1870 or 1871 (there is a dispute as to the precise date). Its first captain was the legendary WG Grace, who held that office for three decades, and during the 1870s the nucleus of the team was provided by the three Grace brothers, WG, EM and GF, all three of whom played in the first Test Match in England in 1880. Between 1873 and 1881 Gloucestershire won the unofficial championship four times (once shared) and were runners-up three times.

Since the reorganisation of the County Championship in 1890, Gloucestershire have never won the title, although they have endured the frustration of finishing second on six occasions. This is surprising in view of the numerous exceptional match-winning players in their teams. Two notable all-rounders at the turn of the 20th century were Charles Townsend, who in 1899 scored 2,440 runs and took 101 wickets with his leg-breaks but thereafter could only devote limited time to cricket owing to his work as a solicitor (and later Official Receiver at Stockton), and the legendary big-hitter Gilbert Jessop. Captain between 1900 and 1912, Jessop led from the front with his unorthodox but mightily effective batting, fast bowling and brilliant cover-point fielding. In 1900 his 2,210 runs and 104 wickets reprised Townsend's rare double of the previous year.

Results, however, were moderate, and remained so until Beverley Lyon became captain in 1929. Although short of pace bowling, Lyon's team included three all-time greats: the incomparable Walter Hammond, the finest English batsman of

Tony Brown on the County Ground, Bristol:

"Ever since my first visit to the County Ground in 1946, aged 10, when I saw Wally Hammond make one of his many 200s, the ground has been one of my favourites. To have been lucky enough to play so many matches on the second-largest playing area in the country has always been a good test of character. And it has been a wonderful experience to follow in the footsteps of such great cricketers as Grace, Jessop, Hammond, Parker and Goddard, all of whom have left indelible marks on the county's history, and then to be able to play with and against some of the great cricketers of my generation on this ground. Although many changes have been made to the ground in recent years, with hopefully more improvements to come, the feeling of history is always there when you walk into the pavilion or out on to the playing area."

Mike Smith on the County Ground, Bristol:

"My overriding memory relates to the size of the ground – how it can seem so small when there is a big crowd. Between 1999 and 2004 we had many big cup semi-finals at the ground with huge crowds. Once the cider started flowing the atmosphere would become electrifying as the regulars in the Jessop Stand got right behind the team. It made a huge difference to our performances."

his generation and (unlike some recent English Test stars) a very heavy run-scorer for his county – he headed the English first-class averages for eight years in a row; and the spinners Charlie Parker and Tom Goddard, who took a combined aggregate of more than 6,000 first-class wickets but shared just nine Test caps between them. In both 1930 and 1931 Lyon's inventive captaincy led Gloucestershire to second place in the Championship.

Goddard's bowling – at the age of 46 he took a county record 222 wickets – helped the club to challenge strongly for the Championship in 1947, but Compton and Edrich's Middlesex were even mightier, winning a crucial match between the two sides by 68 runs despite Goddard taking 15 wickets. In 1959 Tom Graveney led a team notable for its incisive bowling – especially the off-spin of David Brown and John Mortimore – to second place once again.

A decade of decline followed Graveney's removal as captain and his resulting decision to move to Worcestershire, but all-rounder Tony Brown proved to be a doughty captain, leading Gloucestershire to yet another second place in the Championship and, in 1973, to their first trophy, the Gillette Cup. The explosive all-round skills of Mike Procter provided the most telling contribution to the county's successes in that period, so much so that the county was nicknamed "Proctershire". Procter went on to lead the side to the Benson & Hedges Cup in 1977, helped by the silky batting of the prolific Zaheer Abbas.

At the turn of the 21st century, under the captaincy of Mark Alleyne and the coaching of New Zealander John Bracewell, Gloucestershire enjoyed considerable one-day success, winning six trophies in five years. Key to those triumphs were the fast bowling of Mike Smith and Courtney Walsh and the wicket-keeping of the idiosyncratic "Jack" Russell. However, a first Championship title now seems distant, the county having remained in Division Two since relegation in 2005.

Bought and laid out by WG Grace, the County Ground has been Gloucestershire's headquarters for 120 years. Twice, in 1919 and 1976, the club sold the ground, only to buy it back, most recently in 2004. Situated in the northern outskirts of Bristol, it is not the most beautiful of grounds, but has character and space – it has the second largest playing area in English cricket – and is redolent with cricketing history.

THE COUNTY GROUND, BRISTOL

Pavilion

Scoreboard

Pavilion End

Ashley Down Road End

Address The County Ground, Nevil Road, Bristol BS7 9EJ
Main tel 0117 910 8000
Website www.gloscricket.co.uk

Ends Pavilion End, Ashley Down Road End
Capacity 3,600 (15,000 with temporary seating for ODIs)
First County Match Gloucestershire v Lancashire (1 July 1889)
First ODI New Zealand v Sri Lanka (13 June 1983)
Record crowd 16,000 ODI England v India (24 August 2007)

FAMOUS PLAYERS

generally very poor pitches on which he played. A dominant personality, Grace captained Gloucestershire for 29 years until he left the county after an argument in 1899 to establish the London County team at the Crystal Palace. He bought the County Ground in Bristol in 1889.

Tom Graveney

Born in 1927, Tom Graveney was, by common consent, the most elegant batsman of his generation. "If some destructive process were to eliminate all we know about cricket, only Graveney remaining," Sir Neville Cardus once wrote, "we could reconstruct from him every outline of the game… every essential character and flavour contributing to cricket." Graveney played for Gloucestershire from 1948 and captained the side in 1959 (when it was second in the Championship) and 1960.

When the Gloucestershire committee unceremoniously deposed him as captain and appointed in his place the amateur Tom Pugh, who was only a moderate cricketer, Graveney left for Worcestershire, for whom he played with considerable success until 1970 and enjoyed a late re-flowering of his Test career. For Gloucestershire, Graveney scored 19,705 runs (av. 43.02), with 50 of his eventual total of 122 career hundreds.

Two other members of the Graveney family made a significant contribution to Gloucestershire cricket. Tom's brother, Ken, a fast-medium bowler, took all 10 wickets in an innings (10-66) for Gloucestershire against Derbyshire in 1949 – the second-best innings analysis in the county's history – and captained the county in 1963 and 1964. Ken's son, David (see page 17), was a left-arm spin bowler who played for Gloucestershire between 1972 and 1990.

Tom Graveney on College Ground, Cheltenham:
"Certainly Cheltenham is an outstanding ground, belonging to Cheltenham College, where players like Wally Hammond, surely the finest batsman in all conditions, Tom Goddard, Charlie Barnett and many others played. With the ground almost surrounded by tents it has a wonderful atmosphere and is one of the best places to play. When I played there we used to have three 3-day County Championship matches. Many of the crowd take the festival as their summer holidays: they come from all over the country to enjoy the cricket and the town of Cheltenham."

David Allen

David Allen was one of a spin trio who dominated Gloucestershire's bowling attack in the late 1950s and early 1960s, the other two being John Mortimore and "Bomber" Wells. Born in 1935, Allen made his debut for Gloucestershire in 1953, aged just 17, and went on to play for the county for 19 years. An off-spinner, he bowled with a short, four or five pace, run-up. Between 1960 and 1966 Allen played 39 Test Matches for England, and enjoyed success both with the ball and as a late middle-order batsman. There is a satisfying similarity to Allen's first-class and Test records: in first-class cricket he scored almost 10,000 runs and took more than 1,200 wickets, whereas in Tests he scored almost 1,000 runs and took more than 120 wickets.

David Allen on the Winget Sports Ground (formerly known as the Wagon Works ground):
"My favourite ground was the Wagon Works ground at Gloucester, mainly because for many years Charlie Newman, the head groundsman, made the best cricket pitches for both the players and spectators. The pitches would help the opening bowlers on the first day, and the batsmen knew they had to make runs on the second before the spinners came into their own on the third. In 1959 marl was put on the pitch."

Tony Brown

Born in 1936, Tony Brown was captain of Gloucestershire for eight years from 1969, leading the county to its first trophy – the Gillette Cup – in 1973. A central plank of the Gloucestershire team during his long career, Brown was primarily a medium-pacer who opened the bowling, but was also a useful late middle-order batsman, scoring 1,000 runs in the 1964 season, and a fine close fielder, once taking a record-equalling seven catches in a single innings. In 496 first-class matches between 1953 and 1976 he scored 12,851 runs, took 1,230 wickets and held 494 catches. He is now the President of Gloucester CCC.

Mike Smith

Mike Smith (born 1967) was a left-arm fast-medium swing bowler who led the Gloucestershire bowling attack between 1991 and 2004, taking 533 first-class wickets (av 24.68). An important element of the successful one-day team, he took more than 300 wickets in limited-overs cricket. His one Test for England, against Australia in 1997, is an example of how a single event can affect a whole career. In his third over Graham Thorpe dropped an easy catch from Matthew Elliott. Elliott, then on 29, went on to score 199. In contrast Smith ended up wicketless and was never picked for England again.

WG Grace

For almost 150 years WG Grace (1848-1915) has been the face of cricket to the non-cricketing world, his initials and long beard instantly recognisable by people otherwise proud to flaunt their ignorance of the game. From the age of 18 – when he scored 224 not out for England against Surrey – until he marked his 58th birthday with 74 for the Gentlemen against the Players, Dr Grace dominated the cricketing world. During that time he scored almost 55,000 runs, including 126 centuries, took 2,876 wickets with his slow bowling, and took 877 catches (and five stumpings!). His batting feats, which included scores in successive innings of 344, 177 and 318 not out between 11 and 18 August 1876, Test innings of 152 and 170 against Australia and, at the age of 47, 1,000 runs in May 1895, are all the more remarkable in view of the

OTHER GROUNDS

College Ground, Cheltenham *above*

For two weeks in July and August the Cheltenham Cricket Festival takes place on a ground located in the heart of Cheltenham with the famous and picturesque backdrop of Cheltenham College and St Luke's church. The marquees around the ground enhance the charm, although there is little shelter in poor weather.

The annual festival, the most venerable on the county circuit, first took place in 1872. In 1876 WG Grace made what remains the record score on the ground, 318 not out against Yorkshire; the following year, against Nottinghamshire, he took 17 wickets for just 89 runs – still the best match figures at the ground. Equally remarkable all-round feats were performed by Walter Hammond in the 1928 festival. In the first match, against Surrey, he scored 139 and 143, took a world record 10 catches – and bowled out Jack Hobbs. In the next game, he scored 80 after destroying the Worcestershire batting line-up with 9-23 in the first innings and then took a further six wickets in the second.

The Cheltenham Festival has lost the "refined" atmosphere it once had. As writer David Hopps has pointed out, "Those long flowery dresses of officers' wives have given way to bare midriffs of nubile wine-bar girls not long out of one of the local young

ladies' colleges. In early evening, too, throaty male decibels increase – belonging more to Kingsholm than this ground's Gothic chapel."

Archdeacon Meadow, King's School, Gloucester

Between 1993 and 2008 Archdeacon Meadow hosted 15 first-class matches and 11 limited-overs matches. New Zealander Craig Spearman particularly enjoyed batting on the King's School ground. In 2003 he made the highest one-day score on the ground – 153 against Warwickshire – and the following year he broke the 128-year record, held by WG Grace, for the highest first-class score by a Gloucestershire batsman. Spearman made 341 runs off just 390 balls, with 40 fours and six sixes. In September 2008 it was announced that the annual Gloucester cricket festival would cease, owing to commercial pressures, although it is hoped that Twenty20 matches may be played at the King's School ground from 2010 onwards.

Left: Cheltenham; *below:* Archdeacon Meadow, Gloucester;
below left: Archdeacon Meadow, Gloucester

HAMPSHIRE

Hampshire have enjoyed a high-profile in recent years, especially since their move to the Rose Bowl in 2001. The county enjoyed their most successful period in the 1960s and 1970s, winning their first two Championship titles and a number of one-day titles.

Whilst the club was established in 1863, the origins of cricket in the county run a lot deeper. The cricket played there revolved around the Hambledon Cricket Club, which had become a leading side by the 1760s and was integral to the establishment of the county side. Hampshire made their first-class debut in 1864. Though they lost their unofficial first-class status in 1886 after a string of poor results, they returned to the elite of English cricket through their admission to the fledgling Championship in 1895. They struggled at first – in the seasons between 1900 and 1906, for instance, they were usually at the bottom of the Championship.

The dismal run of form was stemmed by an eighth place finish in 1906 under the leadership of EM Sprot. The arrival of prolific batsman Phil Mead and the blossoming of a number of players took the county to a record fifth position in 1914. No one has scored more runs for any county than the 48,892 runs Mead accumulated for Hampshire. His total of 55,061 first-class runs, including 153 hundreds, makes him the fourth highest run-scorer in all first-class cricket. Also in the same team as Mead were Jack Newman and Alec Kennedy, who were consistent all-round cricketers for Hampshire until the 1930s. Another influential figure was Lionel Tennyson (later Lord Tennyson) who arrived in 1913 and was captain from 1919 to 1933. The county's performances picked up; between 1920 and 1930 its average position was 11th, although for

COUNTY RECORDS

Formed in 1863 (admitted to the Championship in 1895)
County Champions 1961, 1973
Gillette/NatWest/C&G/FP 1991, 2005
Benson & Hedges 1988, 1992
Sunday League 1975, 1978, 1986
Twenty20 Best – Quarter-finals 2004
Nickname of one-day team Hawks

Leading run-scorer Phil Mead (1905-36) 48,892 (av 48.84)
Leading wicket-taker Derek Shackleton (1948-69) 2,669 (av 18.23)
Most wicket-keeping dismissals Bobby Parks (1980-92) 700 (630 ct, 70 st)
Most capped England player Robin Smith (1982-2003) – 62 Tests

COUNTY GROUND AVERAGES
Average first innings total in first-class matches 317
Average runs per wicket in first-class matches 28.95
Average runs per over in limited overs matches 4.73

most of the 1930s it gravitated towards the lower reaches of the table.

After the War, Desmond Eagar assumed the captaincy and soon the Hampshire attack was being led by Derek Shackleton and HD Cannings. The attacking left-handed batsman, Colin Ingleby-Mackenzie, came into the side in 1951 and seven years later succeeded Eagar as captain. Under his leadership, Hampshire won their first Championship in 1961, winning 19 out of 32 matches; ten of their victories came from declarations, which was testament to Ingleby-Mackenzie's flair and tactical nous. Substantial contributions were made by Jimmy Gray, Henry Horton and Roy Marshall, all of whom exceeded 2,000 runs, and the indefatigable Shackleton, who took 153 wickets.

Hampshire's second Championship came in 1973, under the leadership of Richard Gilliat, during a successful period for the club which coincided with the recruitment of outstanding

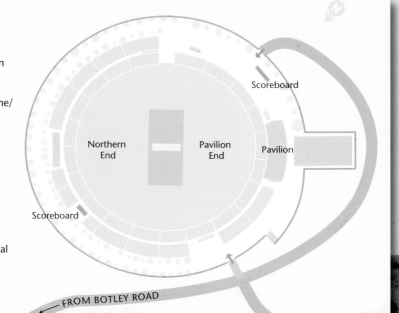

THE ROSE BOWL, SOUTHAMPTON

Address The Rose Bowl
Botley Road, West End, Southampton
Hampshire SO30 3XH
Main tel 023 8047 2002
Website www.rosebowlplc.com/home/
hampshire-cricket

Ends Pavilion End, Northern End
Capacity 9,800 (20,000 with
temporary seating)
First County Match Hampshire v
Worcestershire (9 May 2001)
First ODI South Africa v Zimbabwe
(10 July 2003)
First Test Match Due June 2011
Record crowd 20,000 Twenty20 Final
Kent v Middlesex (26 July 2008)

overseas players including opening batsmen Gordon Greenidge and Barry Richards and paceman Andy Roberts; it also won two one-day league titles in the 1970s. More recently it has continued the tradition of one-day success, with five trophies won in this format between 1986 and 2005. Another West Indian, Malcolm Marshall, made a massive contribution to the earlier of these one-day titles and was a Hampshire stalwart (in 210 first-class matches for Hampshire he took 826 wickets at an average of 18.64 and also scored 5,847 runs). Other key players at the time included Mark Nicholas, who became captain in 1985, and the England batsman Robin Smith.

The county has had several high-profile players in recent times, notably the flamboyant Australian spin bowler Shane Warne (including a spell as captain when he nurtured some of the younger players) and the swashbuckling England batsman Kevin Pietersen. It has also moved to a brand new ground, the Rose Bowl, which has already played host to one-day internationals.

The Rose Bowl, Southampton

Built with the intention of bringing Test cricket to the south coast, the Rose Bowl hosted its first match in 2001, when the visitors were Essex in the Benson & Hedges zonal round. The inaugural first-class match took place soon after, with the visitors being Worcestershire. Perhaps the highlight of the first season at the Rose Bowl for home fans was when the touring Australians were bowled out for 97.

Construction began in 1997, soon after Hampshire had sold its Northlands Road ground and secured £7.2m of Heritage Lottery funding. It is a circular amphitheatre, boasting a three-floor pavilion. Its international debut came when it hosted a match between South Africa and Zimbabwe in 2003. It was the venue for England's first Twenty20 International, played against Australia in 2005, and is due to host its first Test Match in 2011. It has been given strong financial support by businessman Rod Bransgrove, who became Hampshire Chairman in 2000.

OTHER GROUNDS

Chapel Gate Ground, Bournemouth *right*

Hampshire Second XI Championship and Trophy matches are played regularly at the Chapel Gate Ground at East Parley in Christchurch, the home of Bournemouth Sports Club. The ground is located at the south-western end of the main runway at Bournemouth International Airport. The two pitches are pleasantly surrounded by trees. The main pitch has an elevated scoreboard and a large pavilion.

The County Ground, Southampton

The ground at Northlands Road saw its last match in September 2000, having been the home of Hampshire cricket since June 1885, when Hampshire took on Derbyshire. In the course of the 20th century, the stadium expanded to a capacity of 7,000. After Hampshire announced plans to move to a purpose-built new ground, the land at the county ground was sold for redevelopment and it is now a housing estate.

Dean Park, Bournemouth *left*

Established in 1869, this pleasant ground is in the northern suburbs of Bournemouth. The inaugural first-class game was held here in 1897 when the county played the visiting Philadelphians side from the USA. The ground continued to be a regular venue for Hampshire county cricket games until 1992. Now the ground is used by Minor Counties side Dorset.

May's Bounty, Basingstoke

The ground hosted its first match in 1906 and Hampshire matches were played there intermittently until 1966, after which the Basingstoke fixture became a highlight of the Hampshire calendar. The England star batsman Robin Smith took a particular liking to the ground, scoring six centuries there. There are now plans to re-establish first-class games at the venue.

FAMOUS PLAYERS

Phil Mead

The prolific left-hander Phil Mead (1887-1958) was a cornerstone of the Hampshire batting between the Wars. He played for the county from 1905 to 1936, scoring 48,892 runs (av 48.84), more than any other batsman has scored in county cricket, including 138 hundreds. A sound middle-order batsman Mead passed 1,000 runs a season 27 times, twice going on to exceed 3,000 runs. His lack of mobility in the field limited him to 17 Tests, in which he scored 1,185 runs (av 49.37), with four centuries.

Colin Ingleby-Mackenzie

A fast-scoring left-handed batsman, Colin Ingleby-Mackenzie (1933-2006) played for Hampshire between 1951 and 1966 and achieved great success after taking over the captaincy in 1958. In his second season, the team finished second and they soon went one better, winning the Championship in 1961, Hampshire's first major trophy. He had an adventurous captaincy style, and was famed for daring declarations.

David Gower

There were few more pleasing sights in cricket than watching David Gower (born 1957) in full flow at the crease. The elegant left-hander plied most of his county trade for Leicestershire but played the last four years of his career, between 1990 and 1993, for Hampshire, with whom he won the NatWest Trophy in 1991. In August 1992 he played the last of his 117 Tests.

David Gower on Northlands Road, Southampton:
"When I made my move to Hampshire there were all sorts of good reasons to head to Southampton: it was a happy club with a strong squad and a winning habit; I would not have to face Malcolm Marshall, although I would still have to stand at slip for him; and I could bat alongside Robin Smith – it was all good news. The Northlands Road ground was full of Victorian charm, even if the wooden steps up to the home dressing room could be lethal when wet. With the club's success in the one-day game in that era we got some full houses for quarter- and semi-finals and a cracking atmosphere to go with them. Some we won, the odd one we lost. Either way they were special days and I enjoyed playing out my career in such a homely and friendly place."

Tim Tremlett and Chris Tremlett

The Tremletts are a distinguished cricketing family. Tim Tremlett (born 1956), whose father Maurice played three Tests for England and captained Somerset, was a fixture in the Hampshire team from 1976 to 1991. He combined medium-pace bowling with useful lower-order batting, taking 450 first-class wickets, 75 of them in the 1985 season. He toured Sri Lanka with England B but never broke into the full Test squad. On retirement, he became Hampshire coach, then Director of Cricket. His son, Chris (born 1981), made his Hampshire debut in 2000, against New Zealand A. It was an auspicious start for the well-built 6ft 7in bowler, as he took a wicket with his very first ball. Good form for his county led him to make his debut in a one-day international against Bangladesh in 2005 – a successful one, as he took match figures of 4-32, and was denied a hat-trick when the hat-trick ball hit the stumps without dislodging a bail. Tremlett was selected for several England Test squads, including the 2005 series against Australia, but had to wait until 2007 before making his Test debut, against India at Lords, when he took four wickets and became the first Hampshire player born in the county to play a Test in England.

Tim Tremlett on Northlands Road:
"Team pictures from the 1920s that hang in my office show that the County Ground at Northlands Road had not changed dramatically by the time the bulldozers pulled everything down in the winter of 2000. Players and supporters have fond memories of a ground that had its own unique charm despite the fact that it was crumbling at the seams. Returning for pre-season the home dressing-room was a cold, damp space which was warmed by several odd remnants of carpet and a couple of dodgy electric heaters which threw out a modicum of heat. Invariably the showers spluttered into life after a good kick but were seldom warm. We were lucky: the opposition dressing-room was a lot worse in the dungeon positioned underneath and to the back of the main pavilion. Countless great players made a lasting impression at a venue that had some of the best pitches in the country and although modern housing now occupies this sacred site the memories of Shackleton, Richards, Greenidge and Marshall still shine brightly."

Chris Tremlett on the Rose Bowl:
"The Rose Bowl is a fantastic place to play cricket. The pavilion is an amazing site and walking down from the changing room always feels special. The Hampshire crowd appreciate good cricket and are very dedicated fans. The atmosphere at the Rose Bowl when the crowd is full is truly magnificent. My most memorable game at the Rose Bowl took place in 2003 against Glamorgan. After being made to follow on and thanks to some gutsy batting we set them a low target of about 175. On a tough surface on the fourth day we delivered some good and accurate bowling, and bowled them out for under 100 – a great win."

Mark Nicholas

Playing for Hampshire from 1978 to 1995, Mark Nicholas, born 1957, was both a stylish batsman and successful captain for the county. Under his command, Hampshire won four one-day trophies in a successful spell between 1986 and 1992. In 377 first-class matches he scored 18,262 runs at an average of 34.39. Though he played for England A, he was unfortunate never to play a Test for England. He is now a popular television commentator.

Mark Nicholas on the Rose Bowl:
"While creating the Rose Bowl we were acutely aware of the need to retain the unique appeal of Hampshire cricket. Quirky and dated as Northlands Road certainly was, the old ground had an innocence and charm that reflected the various ages of Hampshire cricket. These began in earnest with Lionel Tennyson's captaincy before the modern builders of the club, Harry Altham and Desmond Eagar, paved the way for Colin Ingleby-Mackenzie to bring the county such happiness and style. Since then, most of us have simply hoped to emulate Colin's generosity of spirit and bring with it the character of his winning team. Whatever becomes of the Rose Bowl on its journey to financial independence, the most important thing is that it remains a cricket ground forever associated with the warmth and colour of the people who have given the county its widely respected name."

Derek Underwood

Born in Bromley in 1945, "Deadly Derek" played for Kent from 1963 to 1987. A left-arm bowler who delivered the ball at almost medium pace, he was one of the great spin bowlers of his era. His introduction to county cricket was sensational: he took over 100 wickets in his first season as a 17-year-old. His tally of 297 Test wickets at an average of less than 26 would have been even greater had he not curtailed his Test career by featuring in the Packer World Series and joining a rebel tour of South Africa. He memorably bowled England to victory in the final Test of the Ashes series in 1968, with figures of 7-50. He was a mainstay of the successful Kent team of the era and took over 100 wickets in a season on 10 occasions. When he took his 1,000th wicket in 1970, he was the third youngest player to achieve that feat.

Derek Underwood on the St Lawrence Ground:

"The ground at Canterbury holds many great memories. A special one for me was when Kent were playing against the Australians in 1964. Just as I was about to come on to bowl Colin Cowdrey held up play. Mike Denness ran out on to the field with a cap and Colin presented me with my county cap. The late Norman O'Neill was the second person to shake my hand and congratulate me. What a memory!

To play for Kent in the late 1960s and 1970s during the Festival Week in front of large crowds was a thrill in itself. The ground with its marquees, unique atmosphere and, of course, the only first-class ground with a tree inside the boundary, made it very special. Members would arrive at the crack of dawn to put their cars in their favourite viewing positions. They would rush to reserve their favourite seats. There was always a fantastic atmosphere here for the one-day knock-out matches, with a full house virtually guaranteed."

KENT

With a rich cricketing tradition and great style, Kent have enjoyed two particularly successful periods in their history, between 1906 and 1913 and during the 1970s. Some of the earliest references to the game in England make mention of Kent. In 1610 a match took place at Chevening between teams from the Weald and the Downs. The game became firmly established in Kent from the 17th century and in 1842 Kent Cricket Club was formed.

After its formation in Canterbury in 1842, Kent was the champion county in 1843, 1847 and 1849, but these were unofficial titles. A significant reorganisation took place in Maidstone in 1859 when, following amalgamation with the Canterbury club, Kent CCC was formed. The team started competing in the County Championship when the competition was formalised in 1890.

Lord Harris, who made his Kent debut in 1870, was appointed captain in 1875, and maintained an association with the county for more than 60 years. Kent have enjoyed two particularly successful eras, accumulating seven Championships in the process. During the first of these, between 1906 and 1913, they won four Championships, under the captaincy of Cloudesley Marsham and then Ted Dillon. The prolific side of the early twentieth century benefited from the number of talented cricketers produced by the Tonbridge nursery, which had been set up in 1897. Two of these, Colin Blythe and Arthur Fielder, were to become the most incisive bowlers of the Kent side. In this period, key players included hard-hitting batsman Ken Hutchings and the all-rounder Frank Woolley, who made his debut in 1906.

COUNTY RECORDS

Formed in 1859
County Champions 1906, 1909, 1910, 1913, 1970, 1977 (shared), 1978
Gillette/NatWest/C&G/FP 1967, 1974
Benson & Hedges 1973, 1976, 1978
Sunday League 1972, 1973, 1976, 1995, 2001
Twenty20 2007
Nickname of one-day team Spitfires

Leading run-scorer Frank Woolley (1906-38) 47,868 (av 41.77)
Leading wicket-taker "Tich" Freeman (1914-36) 3,340 (av 17.64)
Most wicket-keeping dismissals Frank Huish (1895-1914) 1,253 (901 ct, 352 st)
Most capped England player Colin Cowdrey (1950-76) – 114 Tests

COUNTY GROUND AVERAGES
Average first innings total in first-class matches 342
Average runs per wicket in first-class matches 34.96
Average runs per over in limited overs matches 4.83

Over the next 32 years, Woolley scored almost 60,000 first-class runs (second only to Sir Jack Hobbs), took over 2,000 wickets and held over 1,000 catches – a record for a non-wicket-keeper.

After the First World War, Kent struggled to maintain their success. While they came close to winning the Championship in 1919, later years were characterised by sporadic brilliance but inconsistency. There were some high-calibre players, such as wicket-keepers Les Ames and Godfrey Evans and the prodigiously talented Colin Cowdrey. Cowdrey first played for Kent in 1950, and was appointed captain in 1956, a position he held until 1971. An elegant batsman, he had a prolific career for England, scoring 7,264 runs in 114 Tests, including 22 centuries.

Kent did not become a consistently successful force in the game again until the 1970s, although in both 1967 and 1968 they finished runners-up in the Championship to Yorkshire. Three further Championships were won in 1970, 1977 and 1978, alongside a string of one-day trophies. These included three Sunday League victories (in 1972, 1973 and 1976) and three Benson and Hedges Cup victories (in 1973, 1976 and 1978). Their success was built on the batting of Cowdrey, Asif Iqbal, Brian Luckhurst and Mike Denness (who was captain between 1972 and 1976) and the wicket-keeping of Alan Knott, as well as the devastating spin-bowling of Derek Underwood. The team have continued to pick up titles, capturing the Sunday League title in 1995 and 2001, and the Twenty20 Trophy in 2007.

The St Lawrence Ground, Canterbury

Canterbury is one of the most idyllic settings for cricket in England. The St Lawrence Ground, which took its name from a nearby hospital founded in 1137, was opened in 1847. In the same year an early Kent team played an All-England team on the ground, and beat them by three wickets. The Canterbury Cricket Week, which takes place in early August, dates from that time. In 1876 the ground was the scene for WG Grace's highest first-class innings, 344 for the MCC against Kent.

The ground was acquired by Kent in 1896 for £4,500. It had been part of the Nackington estate owned by the Earl of Sondes. At the time the only structure on the site was a thatched shed. A

THE ST LAWRENCE GROUND, CANTERBURY

NACKINGTON ROAD

OLD DOVER ROAD

Scoreboard

Nackington Road End

Pavilion End

Scoreboard

Address The St Lawrence Ground Old Dover Road, Canterbury, Kent CT1 3NZ
Main tel 01227 456886
Website www.kentccc.co.uk

Ends Pavilion End, Nackington Road End
Capacity 10,000
First County Match Kent v England (2 August 1847)
First ODI England v Kenya (18 May 1999)
Record crowd 23,000 Kent v the Australians (23 August 1948)

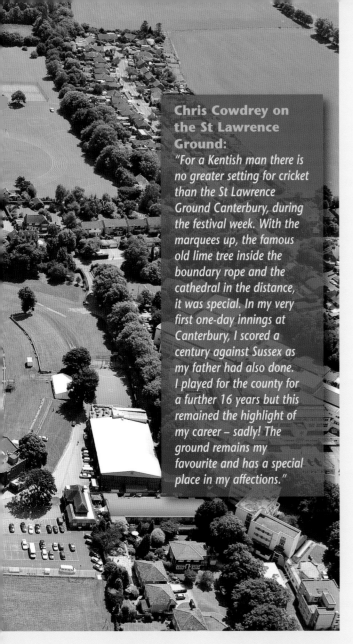

FAMOUS PLAYERS

Derek Ufton

As both a professional footballer and cricketer, Derek Ufton (born 1928) was a rare breed. He made his debut for Kent in 1949 and represented the county over the following 13 seasons. A wicket-keeper, in 149 first-class matches, he made 314 dismissals (270 ct, 44st) and scored 3,919 runs. His football career was arguably more distinguished: he even won an England cap in a showpiece match against the Rest of Europe in 1953. The centre-half played most of his career at Charlton and on retirement was coach and then manager of Plymouth Argyle. More recently he has been involved in the hierarchy of his two primary loves, Charlton FC and Kent CCC.

Chris Cowdrey

As the son of Colin Cowdrey, who played for Kent from 1950 to 1976, Chris was born in 1957 into a cricketing dynasty. He captained England once, in 1988 against the West Indies before picking up an injury. The Cowdreys became the second father and son combination to captain England after Frank and George Mann. Chris Cowdrey played a total of six Test Matches between 1984 and 1988. He was the Kent captain between 1986 and 1990, having made his first-class debut in 1977. In 299 first-class matches, he scored 12,252 runs at an average of 31.90. He retired in 1992 after one season at Glamorgan, and became a radio commentator. His brother Graeme also played as a batsman for Kent.

Alan Knott

Alan Knott came from a tradition of Kent wicket-keeper batsmen, and is one of the finest wicket-keepers England has produced. Born in Belvedere, Kent, in 1946, in his 95 Tests between 1967 and 1978 he made 269 dismissals and amassed 4,389 runs at a healthy average of over 30. His Kent career spanned from 1964 to 1985 and he was an integral part of the county's winning sides of the 1970s. He was renowned for his eccentricities, and for constantly wearing the collar up on his shirt.

Alan Knott on Maidstone:

As a player I liked the fact that there were two dressing-rooms, only one of which was facing the cricket. I always liked to change in the room away from the cricket so that I could fully relax. The wicket was usually quick and bouncy but true. It was the nearest to a Test Match wicket that you could get on a county ground. It helped bowlers with pace and spinners who really spun the ball. I have many fond memories of a ground that seemed to bring me luck. There were always enthusiastic crowds, and for Sunday League games the atmosphere was amazing. In the match at Maidstone against Northamptonshire in July 1966 Keith Andrew, one of my wicket-keeping heroes, told me that he only used wicket-keeping gloves without webbing and asked why, at that time, I chose gloves with webs. I replied that I thought they helped my one-handed catching. I had already taken five catches and a stumping in the Northamptonshire innings when Keith Andrew snicked the ball wide to my right. I dived for the catch, but the ball just squeezed out of the top of the web. Keith turned to me and remarked: 'I see what you mean about the webs!!'"

Aravinda de Silva

Born in 1965, de Silva is one of the finest batsmen Sri Lanka has produced. His one season for Kent, in 1995, is commonly thought to have been a watershed in his cricketing career. Short of stature and an aggressive strokemaker as well as an occasional spin-bowler, de Silva hit a rich vein of form in 1995, hitting 1,661 runs at an average of 59.32 and helping Kent to win the Sunday League and reach the Benson & Hedges final, where it lost to Lancashire despite de Silva's 112. In 93 Tests between 1984 and 2002 he scored 6,361 runs (av 42.97). In the final of the 1996 World Cup he was man of the match, his 3-42 and innings of 107 not out helping Sri Lanka to defeat Australia.

Aravinda de Silva on Canterbury:

"I played for Kent in the 1995 season. I had already been to the ground and played there on the Sri Lankan tour in 1984. It looked totally different to any ground in Sri Lanka because of the tree. This made it special, along with a very good crowd. I was accepted by the supporters at Canterbury just like my home crowd in Sri Lanka. In the 1995 season, I had a bad start to the season but the dressing room was very supportive, and I settled in. While most of my hundreds came at other grounds, I did manage to score a century at Canterbury, a memory I cherish."

was opened in 1900, which was eventually rebuilt ...nded in 1970 when it became the Stuart Chiesman ... (named after the man who was club chairman from ...1968). The ground has a number of stands named ...t heroes, including the Leslie Ames Stand (now ...g of hospitality boxes), the Frank Woolley Stand and ...n Cowdrey Stand, which was completed in 1986 at ...£600,000.

...ost famous landmark associated with the ground is ...located on the outfield. Any shot which hit the tree ...ned a four. Although the original lime tree (thought ...0 years old) blew down in a storm in 2005, another ...planted in March 2005. The historic tree was cleared ...West Indian batsman Carl Hooper in his very first ...or Kent (against Durham in 1994), the third time this ...n to have happened. This picturesque ground has ...a number of one-day internationals, including ...'s victory over Kenya in the 1999 World Cup.

OTHER GROUNDS

Nevill Ground, Tunbridge Wells *right*

Kent played their first match at the Nevill Ground in Tunbridge Wells in 1901, when the opponents were Lancashire. Since then the ground has hosted many Kent matches during the county's renowned cricket festival. It even hosted an international World Cup match during the 1983 tournament, a game still remembered for the Indian all-rounder Kapil Dev's sparkling 175 not out against Zimbabwe. The ground itself is an historic one, having been opened by the Marquess of Abergavenny in 1898, three years after the Tunbridge Wells club moved there.

Mote Park, Maidstone *below*

The first Kent match at Mote Park took place in June 1859 and the county started playing there regularly from 1870. A cricket festival was instituted in 1910 and while the county has not played there in recent years, there is a possibility that it could return to the Maidstone ground.

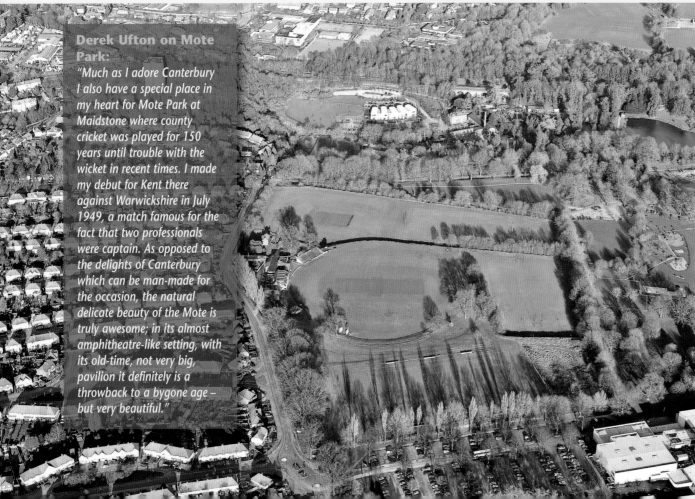

Derek Ufton on Mote Park:
"Much as I adore Canterbury I also have a special place in my heart for Mote Park at Maidstone where county cricket was played for 150 years until trouble with the wicket in recent times. I made my debut for Kent there against Warwickshire in July 1949, a match famous for the fact that two professionals were captain. As opposed to the delights of Canterbury which can be man-made for the occasion, the natural delicate beauty of the Mote is truly awesome; in its almost amphitheatre-like setting, with its old-time, not very big, pavilion it definitely is a throwback to a bygone age – but very beautiful."

Cheriton Road Ground, Folkestone *above*

The county no longer plays at Folkestone – Kent's last match there was against Essex in 1991. Until then, Folkestone Week had been a traditional part of Kent cricket since 1926. The ground, which is close to the North Downs, was opened in 1905. Previously Kent had played at another ground in Folkestone, at Sandgate Hill, from 1862 onwards.

The Kent County Cricket Ground, Beckenham *left*

A clutch of sports grounds surround the Kent County Cricket Ground at Beckenham, seen top right of the photograph with its new white-clad pavilion. The ground dates back to 1918 when Lloyds Bank established a sports club there. In 2004 first-class cricket returned following the construction of a stylish new pavilion. In previous years the ground had been used occasionally by Kent, with one first-class match in June 1954. The new ground is used by Kent's Second XI and for one-day matches.

LANCASHIRE

Lancashire have a proud history stretching back to 1864, the year in which *Wisden* – the cricketer's bible – first appeared, and have produced a series of idiosyncratic characters, many of them brought to life by the pen of Sir Neville Cardus in the *Manchester Guardian*.

The year 1867 saw the first Roses Match against Yorkshire, and the debut of AN "Monkey" Hornby, who made a major contribution to Lancashire's development over the next 50 years, both as a hard-driving batsman, as captain (1880-93 and again, in his early 50s, in 1897 and 1898), and as President between 1894 and 1916. A fine all-round sportsman, he captained England at both cricket and rugby. He formed a famous opening partnership with the ultra-defensive RG Barlow, who carried his bat through an innings 12 times; Barlow once batted for two and a half hours through an innings of 69 all out and ended up with just 5 not out.

Under Hornby, Lancashire won the Championship in 1897, notable contributions being made by slow left-armer Johnny Briggs, fast bowler Arthur Mold and the majestic batsman Archie MacLaren, who two years earlier, against Somerset at Taunton, scored 424 – still the highest score by an Englishman in first-class cricket. MacLaren went on to lead Lancashire to Championship triumph in 1904 without losing a match. The nimble-footed JT Tyldesley and the graceful RH Spooner strengthened the batting; the bowling was led by the mercurial fast bowler Walter Brearley, who took 125 wickets in his 14 Roses Matches.

Lancashire enjoyed a golden era between the Wars, picking up five Championships in nine seasons, three of them, between 1926 and 1928, under the leadership of Major Green in the only years he captained the county. Ted McDonald, the Australian

David Lloyd on Old Trafford:
"My strongest playing memory goes back to 1971 and the so-called 'game in the dark'. It was a Gillette Cup semi-final against Gloucestershire which finished at 8.50pm. The atmosphere at that game will live long in the memory. We came through with David Hughes hitting 26 in one over. Bad light should have stopped play (from our vantage point on the boundary we couldn't see the ball) but there were a lot of people there and we wanted to finish the match. The atmosphere was like a bull-ring! I played for Lancashire at Old Trafford from 1965 to 1983 and I can still almost touch that game. For every player who played at Old Trafford, it made them gel together as a team. In the team I played in, we'd have taken on anybody at home."

paceman with a gliding action, took 484 Championship wickets in those three years, and was supported by the wide-girthed leg-spinner Richard Tyldesley with 303 wickets. A formidable batting line-up was headed by Charles Hallows – who in 1928 scored 1,000 runs in May alone and a county record 11 hundreds – and Ernest Tyldesley, who in 1926 enjoyed a remarkable sequence of a record ten 50s (seven of them centuries) in successive innings. Key contributions to the Championship wins in 1930 and 1934 were made by determined left-hander Eddie Paynter and the all-rounder Len Hopwood.

After the Second World War, Lancashire's batting was dominated by its opening pair, Winston Place and Cyril Washbrook, both of whom passed 2,500 runs in 1947. A shared Championship in 1950 owed much to the spin bowling of Roy Tattersall, who took 153 wickets, and Malcolm Hilton, and the emergence of Lancashire's leading wicket-taker, the exceptionally accurate pace bowler Brian Statham.

Washbrook proved to be a safe but uninspired first professional captain of the county in the mid-1950s. The young Bob Barber almost led Lancashire to the Championship in 1960, a year in which Statham, fellow-paceman Ken Higgs and leg-spinner Tommy Greenhough all exceeded 100 wickets, but the next few years were less harmonious for the county.

A happier era dawned in 1968 with the appointment of Jack Bond as captain. In his five years at the helm, the county won the Gillette Cup three times and the Sunday League twice and challenged for the Championship. Overseas signings Clive Lloyd and Farokh Engineer particularly galvanised the team in the one-day game, with fast-scoring batting from David Lloyd, Barry Wood, Harry Pilling and Frank Hayes and a bowling attack featuring pacemen Peter Lever and Peter Lee and the canny flat off-spin of Jack Simmons.

After a blip in the early 1980s, Lancashire recovered in 1987 to finish runners-up in the Championship, with important batting contributions from Graeme Fowler, Neil Fairbrother and a youngster from Cambridge University, Mike Atherton. Further one-day trophies followed: in both 1990 and 1996 Lancashire carried off the double of winning the Lord's finals of both of the two knock-out competitions. The Pakistani fast bowler Wasim Akram was a formidable weapon.

The Championship crown has, however, proved frustratingly elusive: Lancashire were second again in 1998, 1999, 2000 and 2003, immediately bounced back from relegation in 2004 to promotion as Division Two champions the following year and were Championship runners-up again in 2006. In the final innings of the last game of the 2007 season Lancashire needed to score an improbable 489 to win the Championship. Agonisingly, they were bowled out for 464, to lose the match by 24 runs.

Old Trafford

Old Trafford has been the home of Manchester Cricket Club since 1856 and of Lancashire CCC since its foundation eight years later. Originally leased, the ground was bought from the de Trafford family (from whom the ground's name derives) in 1898 for £24,082. In 1884 Old Trafford became the second ground in England, after The Oval, to host a Test Match. On the second day of the match 12,000 came to see England play Australia. Old Trafford has the reputation of being the wettest of Test grounds. When, in 1890, the Old Trafford Test was completely washed out, RG Barlow complained that "much of this disappointment might have been avoided if my patent wicket protector had been used".

Since then, Old Trafford has hosted many famous Tests. They include the Ashes Tests of 1896, when Ranjitsinhji hit a glorious 154 not out on his Test debut; 1902, when Victor Trumper scored a century before lunch on the first day of the Test and Australia went on to win a thriller by three runs; 1956, when Jim Laker performed his famous, and still unique, feat of taking 19

Bobby Simpson

A prolific opening batsman, a useful leg-break and googly bowler, perhaps the best slip fielder of his generation and a tough captain of Australia, Bobby Simpson's career stretched over 25 years. Born in 1936, his cricketing development was helped by playing in the Lancashire League in 1959 for Accrington, for whom he scored 1,444 runs (av 103.14). As a no-nonsense Australian coach between 1986 and 1996, Simpson built the national side into the strongest team in world cricket. He went on to coach Lancashire in 2000 and 2001.

Bobby Simpson on Old Trafford:

"I always liked the atmosphere of the north – northerners are blunt, a bit like Australians. In 1959 I had a good season playing in the Lancashire League. So it was fitting that it was at Old Trafford that I at long last scored my first Test century. It had annoyed me like hell that I had not scored a Test hundred, but in the Old Trafford Test of 1964 I managed to put that right and went on to make 311. The ground was very slow as there had been a lot of rain before the match, and I scored most of my runs in singles. I reached 300 with a turn around the corner to deep fine leg. That innings played a vital part in my career, as after making my coveted first Test century I went on to score on average a century every three Tests."

Clive Lloyd

Clive Lloyd (born 1944) was a distinctive and commanding presence at the crease, with his stooped 6ft 5in figure, bushy moustache, thick glasses and very heavy bat. He scored more than 7,500 runs in his 110 Tests, with a highest score of 242 not out against India in 1974-75. He was a highly successful captain for 74 Tests, turning the West Indies into the most feared, and most successful, team in world cricket.

Sometimes criticised for failing to curb the bouncer excesses of the fearsome fast bowling quartets at his disposal, he could point to a remarkable run of 26 Tests without a defeat, and led his country to victory in the 1975 and 1979 World Cups, scoring 102 in the 1975 final. Unlike some, his batting thrived on the extra responsibility: whereas he averaged 38.67 in his 36 Tests as non-captain, as captain he averaged 51.30. Lloyd played for Lancashire between 1968 and 1986, captaining the side (albeit with less success than when captaining the West Indies) for four years.

He helped Lancashire to Gillette Cup success in 1972 by scoring 126 against Warwickshire in the final. After spells as West Indies manager and an ICC referee, in 2008 Lloyd became chairman of the influential ICC Cricket Committee.

Clive Lloyd on Old Trafford:

"When I was a kid in Guyana I used to imagine I was playing at Old Trafford. Later I played in the Lancashire League; the next thing I wanted to do was play for Lancashire at Old Trafford. Once I started playing there, Old Trafford took to me like I took to it. I was attracted by the warmth of the people, the atmosphere, the aura of the place, its traditions and history. When we started to do well in one-day cricket, the crowds swelled. We used to attract particularly good crowds for the Bank Holiday Roses Match against Yorkshire. We used to get a lot of the football crowds coming over to support us when the football season was over. There was a lot of chanting and singing – I liked that. The crowds were often very witty.

We played on uncovered pitches – they were often wet or drying out – and that's how I improved my skills. We West Indians were not accustomed to 'sticky dogs'. I had a number of good partnerships at Old Trafford with Harry Pilling. We were a difficult combination for bowlers to bowl the right length to, as he was very short and played a lot off the back foot, and I was very tall and liked to drive off the front foot.

Old Trafford was an old ground when I first played there, but as the team enjoyed success on the field the club improved parts of the ground. The plans have now been passed for a really modern stadium for the 21st century with all amenities."

Australian wickets; and 1981, which featured Ian Botham's dashing century.

Whilst originally amateurs and professionals would walk onto the field at Old Trafford through different gates, in 1902 this tradition was abolished and from then on all went through the same gate, even if they had separate changing rooms.

Old Trafford was used as a hospital during the First World War – over 1,800 patients were treated there by the Red Cross. During the Second World War it was requisitioned by the army and became a transit camp. It suffered severe air-raid damage, and prisoners-of-war helped it to be restored for cricket.

Old Trafford's outmoded facilities have led to the loss of Test cricket until at least 2012, and have prompted a major £200m redevelopment, the first (£12m) phase of which, due to be completed in 2010, will involve the construction of a new banqueting and conference centre, overlooking the pitch, which will be capable of catering for 1,000 people.

The "New Trafford" plans involve a 25,000-seater stadium

OLD TRAFFORD

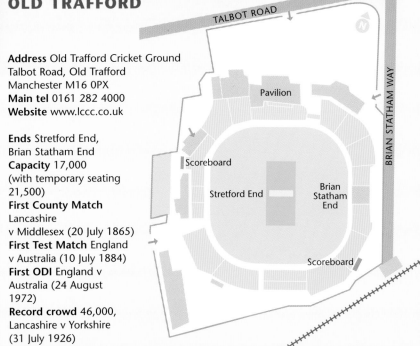

Address Old Trafford Cricket Ground Talbot Road, Old Trafford Manchester M16 0PX
Main tel 0161 282 4000
Website www.lccc.co.uk

Ends Stretford End, Brian Statham End
Capacity 17,000 (with temporary seating 21,500)
First County Match Lancashire v Middlesex (20 July 1865)
First Test Match England v Australia (10 July 1884)
First ODI England v Australia (24 August 1972)
Record crowd 46,000, Lancashire v Yorkshire (31 July 1926)

with permanent floodlights and a complete refurbishment of the pavilion. The wickets are due to be turned at the end of the 2009 season; the players' dressing rooms and media facilities are due to move opposite the pavilion.

FAMOUS PLAYERS

JT & Ernest Tyldesley

The brothers JT Tyldesley (1873-1930, pictured) and Ernest Tyldesley (1889-1962) were the backbone of the Lancashire batting between JT's debut in 1895 and Ernest's retirement 41 years later. To this day they continue to dominate the county's record books. JT's county aggregate for 1901 – 2,633 runs (av 56.02) – remains the most runs made in a season for Lancashire. None has exceeded Ernest's 34,222 runs and 90 centuries for the county (in all, he scored 102 first-class centuries). JT had a long Test career: in an era of talented amateurs he was the only professional batsman of his generation to command a regular England place, which he did for a decade. Nevertheless, his overall Test record – 1,661 runs (av 30.75) – was not outstanding. Ernest, in contrast, was picked only sporadically for England, even though in his 14 Tests he met with considerable success, scoring 990 runs (av 55.00) and three centuries. Fittingly, both made their highest scores at Old Trafford: JT, 295 not out against Kent in 1906, and Ernest, 256 not out against Warwickshire in 1930.

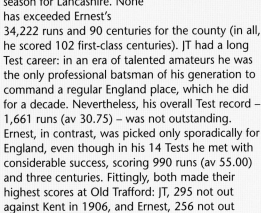

Tommy Greenhough

One of the few leg-break and googly bowlers of his generation, Tommy Greenhough (born 1931) made his debut for Lancashire at just 19, but only reached his peak in 1959 and 1960, when he took, respectively, 122 and 121 wickets. During those two seasons he played four Test Matches, taking 16 wickets (av 22.31), including 5-35 against India in his second Test. His career was subsequently affected by hand injuries and loss of form, and he played his last game for Lancashire in 1965. He ended up with 751 wickets (av 22.37), of which 230 (av 23.03) were taken at Old Trafford.

Farokh Engineer

Born in 1938, Farokh Engineer was an early, and successful, overseas signing, and played for Lancashire as a wicket-keeper batsman between 1968 and 1976. Born in Mumbai, he made his debut for Bombay in 1959-60. He joined Lancashire as an established Test star for India – in January 1967, at Madras, he scored 109, including 94 before lunch on the first day of the Test Match, against a West Indian attack of Hall, Griffith, Gibbs and Sobers – and made important contributions as a quick-scoring batsman in one-day matches. In 46 Tests he scored 2,611 runs (av 31.08) and made 82 dismissals, 16 of them stumpings off the renowned Indian spin quartet of that era. Engineer became a commentator and Test Match referee. As an adopted Lancastrian he lives in the county.

Farokh Engineer on Old Trafford:

"For me Old Trafford is one of the finest and most traditional grounds in the world. I played there for Lancashire between 1968 and 1976. There was a brilliant atmosphere, with a very knowledgeable crowd, who would appreciate good play but could be critical too. On Sundays, such was the demand to come and watch there they would shut the gates. I was fortunate enough to play at Old Trafford in Test Matches but regret that I never got a Test Match hundred there, as I did at my other 'home' ground of Bombay."

David Lloyd

Born in 1947, David Lloyd was an attractive left-handed batsman who made his mark in 1974 by scoring 214 not out against India in only his second Test. But that was the only time he reached 50 in his nine-Test career, which ended after he was shell-shocked by the uncompromisingly aggressive bowling of Lillee and Thomson in Australia the following winter. Lloyd played for Lancashire for 19 years; as captain between 1973 and 1977 he led the county to the Gillette Cup in 1975. In 1983 he signed off with a century in his last match. An under-used left-arm spinner – he boasted best figures of 7-38 – he was also a brave and effective fielder at short-leg. He coached Lancashire to one-day triumphs, was an enthusiastic and chatty England coach between 1996 and 1999, and is now a commentator. His son, Graham, was a fast-scoring batsman who played for Lancashire between 1988 and 2002, representing England in six one-day internationals, two fewer than his father.

Neil Fairbrother

Appropriately named after the famous free-scoring Australian left-handed batsman who retired shortly before his birth in 1963, Neil Harvey Fairbrother played for Lancashire between 1982 and 2002, captaining the county in 1992 and 1993, and scored both heavily and quickly. When he made his highest score, a massive 366, against Surrey at The Oval in 1990, 311 of those runs came in just one day's batting. For someone with a very impressive record in first-class cricket – more than 20,000 runs averaging more than 41, with 47 hundreds – Fairbrother's Test record was unaccountably poor: just 219 runs in 10 Tests, averaging under 16. He was, however, highly successful in his 75 one-day internationals, and in the 1990s was England's premier middle-order batsman in that form of cricket.

Neil Fairbrother on Old Trafford:

"I first played there as an 11-year-old in a youth cricket festival. It was my first foray into the dressing rooms and out on to the field. My bat was almost as big as me. I remember changing at David Lloyd's locker in the dressing room where all these legends had been. Playing there was something I had always dreamed of. It was in 1982 that I made my debut for Lancashire against Kent. I had not expected to play and was at home in bed when the phone rang and it was the Lancashire manager saying they had some injuries and could I play? My Test debut, fittingly, was at Old Trafford against Pakistan in 1987. I went out to bat, with 23 minutes left of play in very dark conditions, to great cheers from my home fans, but returned to the pavilion a few minutes later to deathly silence, having been dismissed for a duck. Playing in front of over 20,000 fans at Old Trafford, whether in a Test Match or a big county match, there is no place quite like it for a Lancastrian."

Ramnaresh Sarwan

Born in 1980, and better known by his nickname Ronnie, Ramnaresh Sarwan is a fleet-footed, attractive stroke-maker, as well as a useful leg-break bowler. He made an immediate mark on Test cricket by scoring 84 not out on his debut, against Pakistan in 2000, but had to wait until his 28th Test – and to endure successive scores against Australia of 0, 0, 2, 1, 0 (and then, to his relief, 51) – before making his first Test century. In June 2004 he made 261 not out against Bangladesh at Kingston, Jamaica. In the 2008–9 series against England he scored over 600 runs, including his highest Test score, 291.

Ramnaresh Sarwan on Old Trafford:

"I like playing at Old Trafford. Playing there is a challenge to both batters and bowlers because the ball tends to do so much. The outfield is lush and good for fielding. In Test Matches the crowd, while supporting England, really appreciate a good performance regardless of whether it is by an English player. In the second innings of the Old Trafford Test in 2004 I top-scored with 60. The West Indies were in a bit of trouble, in difficult conditions, with Harmison and Flintoff bowling very well. Unfortunately my innings was not enough for us to win – we were bowled out for 165 – but the challenging aspect of that situation made me mentally tougher."

Aigburth, Liverpool *left*

Located in the Aigburth district of Liverpool, the Aigburth Road ground has since 1881 been the home of Liverpool Cricket Club, which has a history stretching back more than 200 years. Lancashire played their first match at the ground in 1881, and county matches have been played there regularly ever since. Dating from 1880, the spacious pavilion contains large dressing rooms, bars and much seating. The highest score at Aigburth Road remains Wally Hammond's 264 for Gloucestershire in 1932 – the last of the seven double centuries scored on the ground – and the ground record for best bowling figures has been held since 1920 by AS Kennedy, who took 9-33 for Hampshire. Four years later, Richard Tyldesley destroyed Northamptonshire, his leg-spin yielding remarkable figures of seven wickets for six runs.

Stanley Park, Blackpool *right*

For many years Lancashire played an annual August Bank Holiday fixture at Blackpool's Stanley Park. The cricket ground is located in the western quadrant of Stanley Park, the largest park in Blackpool. Named after Frederick Stanley, the 16th Earl of Derby and a Governor General of Canada, the park is located on land which was donated by the former Blackpool Mayor and MP Sir Lindsay

Parkinson. Unlike Oxford's University Parks, the cricket ground at Stanley Park, which can accommodate 5,000 spectators, is divided from the rest of the park by a wall and trees.

Since 1924 Stanley Park has been the home of Blackpool Cricket Club, whose club professionals have included household names such as Harold Larwood, Rohan Kanhai and Hanif Mohammad. Until 1961 there was a Blackpool festival.

Lancashire stopped playing at Stanley Park in 1978, but an annual fixture resumed 10 years later.

Notable cricketing feats performed at Stanley Park include Mike Atherton's highest first-class score – a ground-record 268 not out for Lancashire against Glamorgan in 1999 – and Lancashire spinner Bob Berry's taking all 10 wickets (for 102 runs) against Worcestershire in 1953.

Tommy Greenhough on Stanley Park, Blackpool:
"Being an ex-Lancashire player I had a great fondness for Old Trafford. Away from Old Trafford I used to love playing at Blackpool. The atmosphere was very pro-Lancashire at this lovely seaside ground. I usually did well there. I remember in 1959 Jim Stewart of Warwickshire hit 17 sixes. The pro-Lancashire crowd enjoyed it all. I did OK. I took 5-79 in the first innings, but then I pulled a muscle, which left me missing the next three matches."

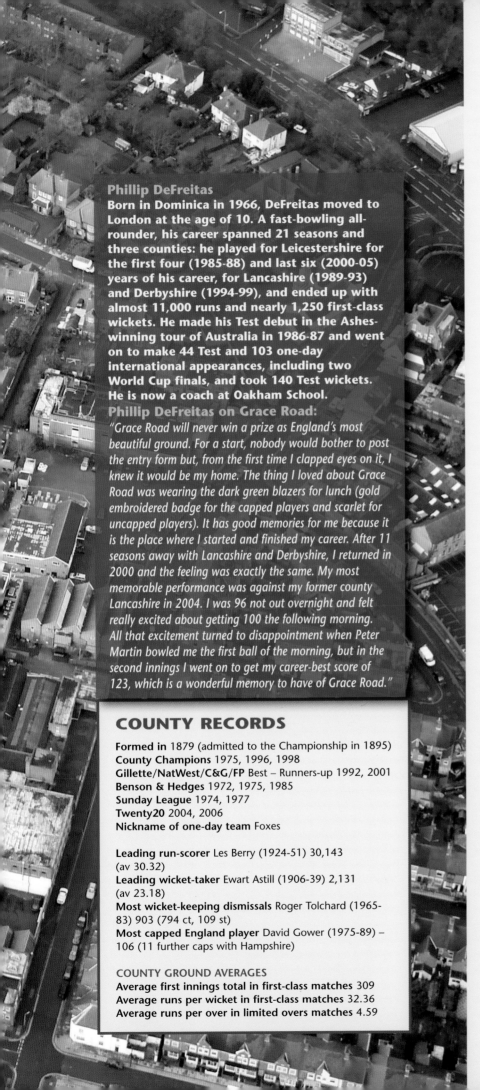

LEICESTERSHIRE

Cricket became popular in Leicestershire as early as the 18th century. Local craftsmen did "piece" work in their own homes, and so could devote their afternoons to playing and watching cricket. In 1878 the Grace Ground, covering some 16 acres, was opened. The present county club was formed the following year. Leicestershire performed well in the second-class championship – in 1888 it won the championship and defeated the touring Australians – and in 1895 joined the County Championship.

Under the captaincy of the big-hitting CE de Trafford, Leicestershire finished fifth in 1905. That result was not improved upon for almost 50 years despite the patient batting of CJB Wood, who carried his bat through an innings on 17 occasions; the all-round skills of JH King, who at the age of 52 scored 205 against Hampshire; and the tireless Ewart Astill and George Geary. The latter two effectively were the county's bowling attack in the 1920s and early 1930s. Astill ended up with more wickets (2,131) than any other bowler for the county – as well as scoring over 22,000 runs in his career – and in 1935 became the first professional captain of any county in the 20th century. Geary, who bowled appreciably quicker than Astill, once had the remarkable innings figures of 10-18 against Glamorgan.

After the Second World War, for three years the prolific opening bat Les Berry, who scored more runs and centuries for the club than anyone else, was captain. However, the county's revival came with the recruitment of Charles Palmer, who was an inspiring captain between 1950 and 1957. A hard-hitting middle-order batsman and medium-paced bowler who once took eight

Surrey wickets for seven runs, Palmer led Leicestershire to third place in 1953. The mainstays of the team were the excellent Australian all-rounders Vic Jackson and Jack Walsh.

Leicestershire's policy of recruiting experienced players from other counties to captain the side bore fruit first with the former Yorkshire batsman Willie Watson (captain 1958-1961), then with the forthright Tony Lock, who led the county to joint second place in 1967 and, most of all, with Ray Illingworth (captain 1969-1978). An astute, Ashes-winning England captain, Illingworth was also a canny off-spinner and a good enough batsman to score more than 24,000 runs in his career.

In partnership with secretary manager Mike Turner, Illingworth led Leicestershire to its first trophy – the Benson & Hedges Cup – in 1972, the Sunday League followed in 1974 (and again in 1977) and in 1975 came the notable double of the Benson & Hedges Cup and the county's first ever Championship. Substantial contributions were made by batsmen Brian Davison, Chris Balderstone, Barry Dudleston and John Steele: in 1979 the latter two shared an opening stand of 390, the club's highest partnership ever in county cricket.

In 1985 the elegant left-hander David Gower led Leicestershire to a further Benson & Hedges Cup, assisted by the gritty all-rounder Peter Willey and the fast bowling of Jonathan Agnew. After being runners-up in 1994, further County Championship titles followed in 1996 and 1998. These were team efforts, under captain James Whitaker and coach Jack Birkenshaw, who had previously made notable all-round contributions to Illingworth's triumphs in the 1970s. However, success could not be sustained. Since 2004 Leicestershire have been in the second division of both the County Championship and the Sunday League. Despite the determined captaincy of Paul Nixon and the batting of Hylton Ackerman – who in 2006 scored the second triple century ever for the club – results have not improved. Two Twenty20 Cup trophies have been insufficient consolation.

Grace Road, Leicester

In 1877 the Leicestershire County Cricket Ground Co Ltd purchased 16 acres of land from the Duke of Rutland and laid out the Grace Road ground. The following year, an estimated 30,000 spectators watched the Australians play Leicestershire. Subsequently, crowds at Grace Road tended to be small, as it was far from Leicester town centre and had poor transport links – only horse trams came to Grace Road. As a result, the county moved to the more central Aylestone Road ground in 1901 and sold Grace Road.

When, in 1945, the club's lease on Aylestone Road (which had been damaged during the war) was not renewed, the county returned again to Grace Road. At that time the ground was owned by the local education authority and was used as a school sports ground: from the roof of the pavilion the markings of football and rugby pitches could be seen on the outfield. The ground's playing and watching conditions were very poor until it was gradually redeveloped after being bought by the club in 1966, with a new pavilion, indoor school, media centre and museum. The redevelopment of the ground led to Grace Road hosting one-day internationals for the first time. What was formerly known as the Hawkesbury Road End is now the Bennett End, in recognition of the benefactor Trevor Bennett MBE. Leicestershire possess a fabulous indoor cricket school, the Mike Turner Cricket Centre, which also contains lecture rooms and a media centre.

David Gower on Grace Road:

"The Grace Road of my day boasted a beautiful true pitch with a well-manicured, quick outfield, a combination that made for plenty of runs and some well-judged declarations if a result was to be achieved in the Championship and for some high-scoring one-day matches. There was always a hard core of support at Grace Road but when the team stirred itself to proper action the crowds would swell. One of the hard core was a man known only as 'Foghorn', who would leave his terraced house on the Milligan Road just after the start of play every day, announcing from outside the ground in his stentorian tones, 'I'm coming'. Once in the ground he would issue a constant stream of instructions to the captain, again in that foghorn voice, many of which were acutely judged. Ray Illingworth often found himself having to abandon the perfect tactic for a moment only because it could have appeared that he was following instructions from the boundary edge! In those days the pavilion was the most comfortable part of the ground, the home dressing-room cunningly more spacious than the visitors', and when the sun shone – those were the days! – the balcony was the perfect place from which to watch if one was unlucky enough to have failed with the bat. It was always a functional ground, lacking some of the charm of, say, Canterbury or Hampshire's old Northlands Road ground, but to me it was home and a happy one at that."

GRACE ROAD, LEICESTER

Address The County Ground, Grace Road, Leicester LE2 8AD
Main tel 0871 282 1879
Website
www.leicestershireccc.co.uk

Ends Pavilion End, Bennett End
Capacity 6,000
First County Match
Leicestershire v Yorkshire
(17 May 1894)
First ODI India v Zimbabwe
(11 June 1983)
Record crowd 6,000 Twenty20
Quarter-final Leicestershire v
Kent (24 July 2006)

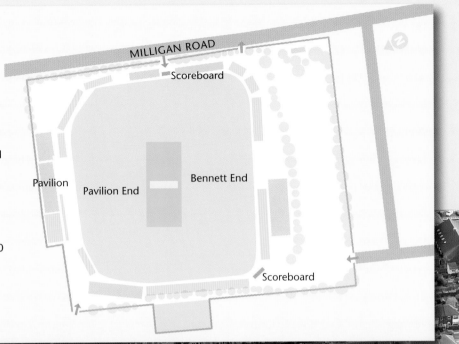

OTHER GROUNDS

Oakham School, Oakham *above & right*

In 2000 county cricket returned to Oakham School, after a gap of some 60 years. That match, against Surrey, saw the highest score ever made at the ground – Ali Brown's hard-hit 295 not out. In contrast, the best innings bowling figures on the ground – 8-123 – were taken by the diminutive Kent leg-spinner "Tich" Freeman as long ago as 1935.

The Oakham School ground had previously been used for Leicestershire Second XI's matches. The cricket ground is that of a public school founded in 1584 whose alumni include Stuart Broad, the England all-rounder, and the former England women's fast bowler Lucy Pearson.

FAMOUS PLAYERS

George Geary

George Geary (1893-1981) was, until David Gower, Leicestershire's most illustrious cricketer. The first of 16 children of a shoemaker, he played for the club between 1912 and 1938. A useful batsman, he scored three centuries in his last season, when he was 45. But his main fame was for his fast-medium bowling, which incorporated seam, spin and "cutters". He played 14 Test Matches, taking 46 wickets, including 12 (7-70 and 5-60) against South Africa in Johannesburg in 1927-28. Famed for his perseverance and accuracy, he once bowled 81 overs in an innings against Australia, giving away just 105 runs for his five wickets. Geary ended up with 2,063 wickets. He ruined his own benefit match in 1936 by taking 7-7 and 6-20: because the game ended early the match yielded him just £10. After retirement he became a renowned coach at Charterhouse.

Jack Birkenshaw

One of several Yorkshiremen of his era – including Willie Watson, Ray Illingworth and "Dickie" Bird – who revitalised their careers by moving to Leicestershire, Birkenshaw (born 1941) was a right-arm off-break bowler and a left-handed middle-order batsman. After playing for Yorkshire between 1958 – he made his debut at the early age of 17 – and 1960, Birkenshaw moved to Grace Road, where he was an important figure as a player for two decades and later – after a spell as a Test umpire – as the county coach. In 490 first-class matches he scored 12,780 runs and took 1,073 wickets. He is currently assistant coach to the England Women's cricket team, which won the 2009 World Cup.

Jack Birkenshaw on Grace Road:
"When I joined Leicestershire in 1961 Grace Road was one of the worst grounds in the Championship. Not many players showered because of the danger of falling down in the steep incline that led to the showers. Over the years there have been massive improvements. Grace Road is now the most improved ground in the country. Mike Turner did well in developing the net area of the ground – which used to house tennis courts – into the best cricket nets in the country. When Tony Lock captained Leicestershire, he made sure that the pitches were good for the spinners. Once when we played Essex, a lot of sand had been thrown on the pitch on a good
length. To register a protest, on the first morning of the match Trevor Bailey, the Essex captain, took a deckchair onto the pitch and sat there with a bucket and spade for several minutes. But the game went on."

Graham McKenzie

Born in Perth in 1941, Graham McKenzie was a fast bowler noted for his smooth bowling action and stamina. After destroying England with five for 37 on his Test debut at Lord's in 1961, he became the linchpin of the Australian bowling attack for the next decade. He ended up with 246 wickets in 60 Tests, 73 of them taken in the year between December 1963 and December 1964. McKenzie played for Leicestershire between 1969 and 1975, and contributed significantly to the county winning the Championship in his last season. In 76 matches at Grace Road, he took 223 wickets (av 22.39).

Graham McKenzie on Grace Road:
"I first played at Grace Road for the Australians in 1961, when I was 19. I took my first five-wicket haul in first-class cricket in Leicestershire's first innings: this helped me to gain selection for my Test debut at the following week's Lord's Test. My experience as a pace bowler was that Grace Road was not my favourite ground to play on during my seven seasons with Leicestershire. It was a good wicket but not generally conducive to seam or pace to a great degree, particularly in the second innings. Often the spinners came into the game much more as the game progressed. But we fast bowlers had our moments. When we played Glamorgan in August 1971 it had rained quite a bit, but the ground had missed out on the rain, so I was disappointed. After I bowled the first over of the morning I went down to fine leg and told a spectator that the conditions were not as good as the day before when the ball moved around: I was not optimistic. But we got Glamorgan out for 23, and I took seven for 8: it would have been seven for 4 but Peter Walker snicked one through the slips for four! It was one of those days when almost everything went right."

David Gower

Born in 1957, at the age of 21 David Gower made an immediate impact on Test cricket, pulling the first ball he received for four. The supremely elegant left-handed batsman was a mainstay of the England team for 117 Tests. As laid-back as captain as he was languid as a batsman, he led England to an Ashes triumph

in 1985 – scoring 732 runs in the series – but results were far less successful in subsequent series against the West Indies and Australia.

A man for the big stage, Gower's Test record of 8,231 runs (av 44.25) was far more impressive than his figures for Leicestershire: 10,685 runs (av 38.99). But he led the county to the Benson & Hedges Cup in 1985 and so entertained its supporters that, despite the fact that he spent the last four years of his career at Hampshire, in 2000 the new executive suite at Grace Road was named after him.

Paul Nixon

Paul Nixon (born 1970) has been Leicestershire captain since 2007. He has played for the club since 1989, save for three years with Kent. At the age of 36 his bubbly enthusiasm led him to be called up for England in one-day cricket in Australia and then for the World Cup in 2006-7, when he scored a total of 193 runs off 194 balls. For Leicestershire, he has often been the most consistent batsman, scoring 2,728 (av 53.49) between 2006 and 2008 in first-class cricket and many more runs in one-day and Twenty20 matches, especially with his powerful reverse-sweep.

Paul Nixon on Grace Road:
"I remember walking into the ground at Grace Road as a 17-year-old on trial against Warwickshire with the great Allan Donald flying down the hill with the new ball – this is proper cricket, I thought. Over the years the many friends mixed in with legends of the game such as Gower, Willey, Winston Benjamin, Agnew and DeFreitas have all made a huge impact on the club. Tight games to the wire plus unique victories: one that stands out was when we needed 204 in 20 overs in a Championship game v Northants and won! I warmly remember the 1996 victory against Middlesex and winning the County Championship, and the festivities and celebrations that followed the conga round the ground with players and supporters together. I am now proud to lead a new generation towards their own very special memories."

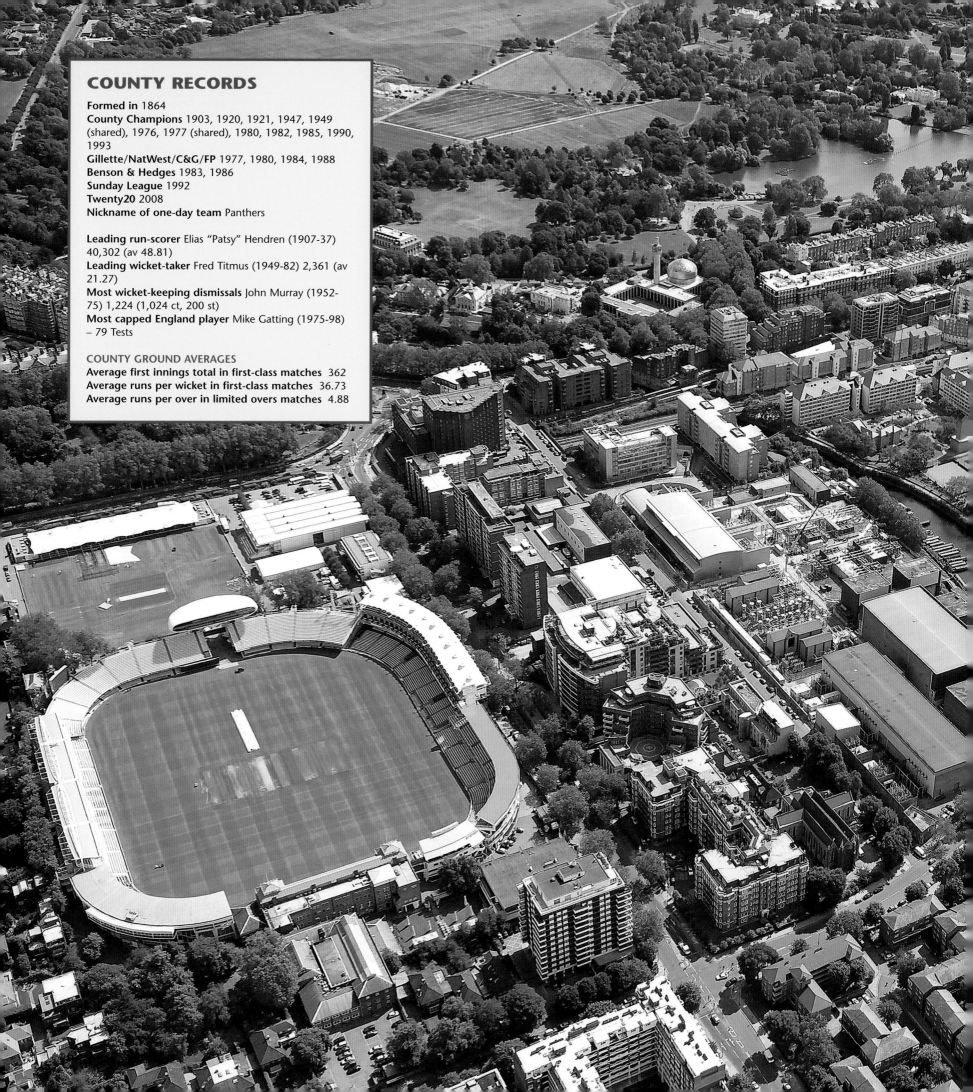

COUNTY RECORDS

Formed in 1864
County Champions 1903, 1920, 1921, 1947, 1949 (shared), 1976, 1977 (shared), 1980, 1982, 1985, 1990, 1993
Gillette/NatWest/C&G/FP 1977, 1980, 1984, 1988
Benson & Hedges 1983, 1986
Sunday League 1992
Twenty20 2008
Nickname of one-day team Panthers

Leading run-scorer Elias "Patsy" Hendren (1907-37) 40,302 (av 48.81)
Leading wicket-taker Fred Titmus (1949-82) 2,361 (av 21.27)
Most wicket-keeping dismissals John Murray (1952-75) 1,224 (1,024 ct, 200 st)
Most capped England player Mike Gatting (1975-98) – 79 Tests

COUNTY GROUND AVERAGES
Average first innings total in first-class matches 362
Average runs per wicket in first-class matches 36.73
Average runs per over in limited overs matches 4.88

MIDDLESEX

With the glamorous Lord's as its home ground, Middlesex has always been a prestigious county. The club's founding family were the seven Walker brothers, all of whom played for a north London side. In 1859 the Walkers were instrumental in arranging for a team called "Middlesex" to play Kent. The county was officially founded in 1864, playing their first match against Sussex in Islington. They had a precarious period in the late 19th century, nearly closing after a committee vote to remain in existence was passed by 7 votes to 6. The link between Middlesex and Lord's dates from 1877 when the owner of Lord's, the Marylebone Cricket Club, invited the county to become its tenant.

Middlesex's success in the County Championship dates back to the early twentieth century. They first won the title in 1903 and, while consistent success was hampered by a high number of amateur players, they won the Championship again in 1920 under the leadership of "Plum" Warner. The strong batting line-up featured Harry Lee, Jack Hearne and "Patsy" Hendren, a much-loved man who ended up with more runs and centuries for Middlesex than anyone else; Hearne, with 123 wickets, and paceman Jack Durston provided the backbone for the bowling attack, which also featured the leg-spin of the teenage GTS Stevens. The finale to the season was dramatic, with Middlesex beating Surrey at Lord's by 55 runs in the last hour of the game to carry them to the Championship. That was Warner's last match for Middlesex: he retired, at the age of 46, having been captain since 1908. His replacement as skipper, Frank Mann,

promptly led Middlesex to the 1921 Championship crown.

For the remainder of the 1920s and the 1930s, further Championship success eluded Middlesex, under the captaincy of Mann and Nigel Haig. However, their next title-winning season was particularly memorable. In the glorious 1947 season the "Terrible Twins", Denis Compton and Bill Edrich, between them scored a remarkable 7,355 runs and 30 centuries, and took 140 wickets. With the openers Robertson and Brown both passing 2,000 runs, Middlesex marched towards the Championship under the ever-attacking leadership of Walter Robins despite not possessing a particularly strong bowling attack.

Although Middlesex shared the title with Yorkshire in 1949 – the first time that the honour was shared since the Championship began in 1890 – the county struggled to live up to these heights for most of the following 25 years (for example

finishing between fifth and seventh in every season between 1951 and 1957), despite the significant contributions of the off-spinning all-rounder Fred Titmus, wicket-keeper John Murray and batsman Peter Parfitt.

The most successful era in the club's history occurred from 1976 onwards under the canny leadership of Mike Brearley, captain since 1971. The 1976 team featured the batting of Graham Barlow and a youthful Mike Gatting and the spin bowling of Titmus, in the last full year of his illustrious career, and the young Phil Edmonds. The Championship was won five times in the decade that followed, and the team also picked up several one-day trophies during this time.

Mike Gatting, who took over from Brearley as captain in 1983, continued the run of success. He was helped by a strong pace attack, featuring Wayne Daniel and Norman Cowans and batting

INTERNATIONAL VIEWPOINT

John Reid

Born in 1928, John Reid was a powerfully-built big-hitting all-rounder who captained New Zealand in 34 Tests between 1956 and 1965. After retirement, he went on to become a New Zealand selector and an international match referee. His son Richard played nine one-day internationals for New Zealand between 1988 and 1991.

John Reid on Lord's:

"Lord's is my favourite ground. The tradition, history and atmosphere make it to my mind the ultimate cricket ground. I first played at Lord's in 1949. I was very disappointed never to score a century at headquarters. I had an ideal opportunity playing for the New Zealanders against Middlesex in 1965, when I made a basic error in trying to run an off-break from Fred Titmus down past gully. The ball came back off the slope and bowled me for 97. I kicked myself for my mistake. Lord's was also the ground where in 1965 I captained the Rest of the World XI against an England XI, with Garry Sobers as my vice-captain. My team included greats such as Wes Hall, Charlie Griffith and Rohan Kanhai. As captain of New Zealand I had been used to giving the team a pep talk before going on the field but with the Rest of the World XI I remained very quiet. The team arrived at the ground just 20 minutes before play; there was no warm-up; but the first ball of the match, bowled by Wes Hall, came down like a thunderbolt – and made me take notice, fielding at gully!"

Alan Davidson

Alan Davidson (born 1929) was a fast-scoring lower-order batsman, a wonderful fielder both close in and in the deep and, most of all, a penetrative left-arm opening bowler, famed for his accuracy. His economy rate in Test cricket was 1.97 runs per over, comparing favourably with any fast bowler in Test cricket. He played for New South Wales from 1949 to 1963 and took 186 wickets in 44 Tests at the fine average of 20.53.

Alan Davidson on Lord's:

"One of the rather unique things about Lord's is that in order to get onto the ground you need to walk down the stairs, through the Long Room and down the pavilion steps – you almost have to do a route march before you reach the playing area. Just think how many great players have traced those steps over the past 150 years – including WG Grace, Trumper and Bradman! You can actually see the sprig-marks that they made on the pavilion floor! All this creates a real aura. Lord's is where cricket really started and so it has great significance. That's why Australians regard Lord's as the home of cricket and always want to play there. That's also why Australians often tend to lift themselves above their normal game when playing there: in the last 110 years we have only lost one Lord's Test."

The Lord's crowd is very cosmopolitan, and always acknowledges good play. In the second Test at Lord's, in 1953, I had reached 76 when Godfrey Evans, the England wicket-keeper, sledged me out. He asked me: 'Have you ever scored a century at Lord's?' Of course I hadn't, as this was my first Test there, but it broke my concentration. I hit the next ball, from Alec Bedser, down the throat of Brian Statham at mid-off! In the 1961 Lord's Test I took 5-42 and we won what was an exciting and low-scoring Test."*

Bevan Congdon

Bevan Congdon (born 1938) was a New Zealand all-rounder who played 61 Test Matches between 1965 and 1978. In Test cricket, he scored 3,448 runs (av 32.22), whilst his useful medium-pace bowling brought him 59 wickets. When necessary, Congdon could bat aggressively, and in his 11 one-day internationals he boasted an impressive average of 56.33.

Bevan Congdon on Lord's:

"The ambition of New Zealand cricketers is to succeed, and to gain selection on a tour to England – at least in part because of the long gaps between tours. While this has changed to some extent with modern cricket scheduling, I was very fortunate to tour England four times. I achieved one of my personal goals – to play at Lord's. I did so a number of times and I have been left with great memories of the ground and of my own performances there. The century on my first appearance, against the MCC, and a Test century when captaining New Zealand are special to me, in view of the tradition and atmosphere of playing at Lord's – the acknowledged home of cricket."

Aron "Ali" Bacher

Born in 1942, Bacher was a talented batsman who, at 21, became the youngest-ever captain of Transvaal. He went on to captain South Africa. Bacher made his Test debut at Lord's in 1965. Following the end of his playing days, Bacher practised as a doctor and became an influential cricket administrator. He organised the rebel tours of South Africa in the 1980s, and in the post-apartheid era headed the South African United Cricket Board for a decade from 1992. His nephew Adam Bacher played 19 Tests for South Africa in the late 1990s.

Ali Bacher on Lord's:

"My first Test Match was played at Lord's. We won the toss and decided to bat first. I have never been so nervous in my life – probably because of the history of the game at Lord's. So nervous that I could not even watch play from the opposition balcony. I eventually convinced

myself that this was another game. When it was my turn to bat I sauntered on to the field, quite relaxed with no adrenalin pumping, and when that happens in Test cricket there is only one outcome – a quick return to the dressing room."

Ramiz Raja

The younger brother of Wasim Raja, a fine all-rounder who played 57 Tests for Pakistan between 1973 and 1985, Ramiz Raja (born 1962) made his first-class debut in 1978. Consistent scoring as an opening batsman in Pakistani domestic cricket paved his way to the national side. In 1984, in his debut against England at Karachi, he made scores of 1 and 1. Despite this early setback, he went on to play 57 Tests over 13 years, with two centuries. He captained Pakistan for a brief time, in 1995-96. As an international player he was more successful in the one-day game, playing 198 ODIs and scoring nearly 6,000 runs with nine centuries. He took the catch which dismissed the last English batsman to win the 1992 World Cup Final. His highest first-class score was 300. Following retirement, he became a well-respected cricket commentator, and combined this for a time with the role of chief executive of the Pakistan Cricket Board.

Ramiz Raja on Lord's:

"Lord's is the Mecca of cricket. And I am proud to have made the pilgrimage. I remember being at Lord's and acting like a country boy, gawping at the princely structure of its pavilion. The graceful Long Room, the glacial faces of the members occupying it, and, outside, the billiard table-like smooth silken grass were all asking me just one question: do you deserve to be here? I was overwhelmed with emotion. Walking through the famous Grace Gates was like walking down the galaxy lane. All of those great cricketers of the past would have walked the same route to the ground. They would have walked up and down the same stairs and shared the same dressing room. You felt lifted and transported to a surreal world. Lord's is like tracing the genesis of cricket.

I was involved with two memorable games at Lord's. One was the Test Match in 1992 which we narrowly won. Although I sat out that game because of injury, it was such a nail-biter that at the end of it I felt emotionally and physically drained as if I had hit the winning runs! The other was a one-day game on the same tour. We had to defend a small total, which we managed to do. Javed Miandad was the captain, but he got injured during his innings. I led in his place and to date it ranks among my favourite games."

based upon the openers Graham Barlow and Wilf Slack, as well as the veteran Clive Radley. Championship titles followed in 1990 and 1993, with the West Indian opener Desmond Haynes and Mark Ramprakash mainstays of the batting. However, since then the club's high standards have dipped, even though it has continued to supply a number of players to the England team and a return to the glory years was hinted at by the Twenty20 victory in 2008.

Lord's, St John's Wood

Lord's is quite simply the most famous and prestigious cricketing venue in the world. Described as the "home of cricket", it is where every young cricketer around the globe dreams of playing. As an international cricketing venue,

LORD'S, ST JOHN'S WOOD, LONDON

Address Lord's Cricket Ground
St John's Wood Road, St John's Wood,
London NW8 8QN
Main tel 020 7289 1300
Website www.middlesexccc.com

Ends Pavilion End, Nursery End
Capacity 28,000

First County Match Middlesex v MCC
(31 May 1815)
First Test Match England v Australia
(21 July 1884)
First ODI England v Australia (26 August 1972)
Record crowd 27,835 Australia v Pakistan
(World Cup Final, 20 June 1999)

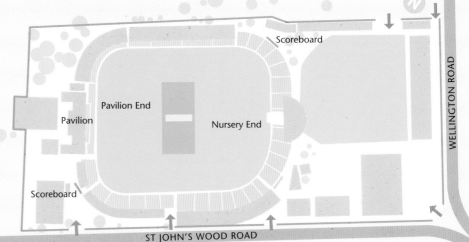

Lord's has an iconic status comparable to Wembley in football or Twickenham in rugby. It has hosted over 100 Test matches, four World Cup Finals and English domestic cricket finals for four decades.

Lord's was not always located on the present site. It was named after its owner Thomas Lord, a Yorkshire businessman. Originally, from 1787, it was based in the area known as Dorset Square (in London's West End); it then moved to Regent's Canal, near its present location, in 1811 before moving for the last time in 1814. The ground has been privately owned by the Marylebone Cricket Club since 1866, and started playing host to Middlesex in 1877.

The architecture of the ground is a mixture of the traditional and modern. The pavilion was built in the Victorian era, designed by architect Thomas Verity and completed in 1889-90. Directly opposite the pavilion, which contains the famous Long Room, is the Media Centre at the Nursery End, which was opened in 1999. The spectator stands include the Warner Stand (named after "Plum" Warner and opened in 1958), the Compton and Edrich Stands and the Tavern Stand, which dates from 1967. Other more recently constructed stands are the Mound Stand (1987) and the main Grandstand (1997).

"Old Father Time", Lord's famous weathervane, was moved from the old Grand Stand when that stand was demolished to the other end of the ground in 1996. Over the last 20 years Lord's has been extensively modernised, and £50m has been spent on redevelopment since 1987. There are further plans to develop the venue, with the intention of increasing the capacity and improving the "Lord's experience" for all spectators.

Great cricketing moments

The ground, located in the St John's Wood area of London, hosted the first three World Cup Finals, in 1975, 1979 and 1983, and again in 1999. It plays host to the Twenty20 World Cup Final in 2009 and will again stage the longer-format one-day World Cup Final in 2019.

Lord's first hosted a Test Match against Australia in 1884. Since then it has showcased the greats of the game, witnessing some amazing achievements along the way. In 1899 the all-rounder Albert Trott, playing for the MCC against the touring Australians, hit Monty Noble over the pavilion at Lord's, the only time the landmark has been cleared. Another Australian, Bob Massie, made a remarkable debut at Lord's in 1972, taking match figures of 16-137 against England (Massie was to play only five more Tests). The 1990 England-India Test Match featured a number of records, with Graham Gooch scoring 333 and 123, and Kapil Dev hitting four consecutive sixes off Eddie Hemmings to help India avoid the follow-on. Lord's continues to be the ground where every international cricketer dreams of an outstanding performance and harbours ambitions to have his name engraved on the honours boards.

As befitting a place nicknamed "headquarters", Lord's contains the head office of the English Cricket Board (the ECB) and was, until 2005, also the headquarters of the International Cricket Council. It is due to host the archery tournament at the London 2012 Olympics.

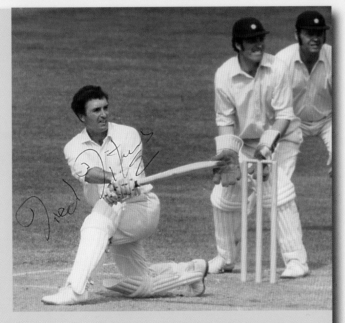

Fred Titmus

One of a select group of men who played first-class cricket in five decades, Fred Titmus (born 1932) played for Middlesex between 1949 and 1982, his off-breaks taking 2,361 wickets for the county, a Middlesex record. He took 100 wickets in 16 seasons and, a brave middle-order batsman, in eight of them also scored 1,000 runs. Titmus played 53 Tests for England, scoring almost 1,500 runs and taking 153 wickets, at a time when there was a glut of high-quality spinners in the country. Overcoming a terrible accident on the England tour of the Caribbean in 1968 when four of his toes were severed, Titmus was restored to the England team for the 1974-75 tour of Australia, where, aged 42, in the first Test he top-scored with an innings of 61 against the pace of Lillee and Thomson. Titmus retired after making a significant contribution to Middlesex's 1976 Championship triumph, but continued to make sporadic appearances, the last in 1982; when attending a Middlesex v Surrey match as a spectator, he was called on by Middlesex captain Mike Brearley and bowled Middlesex to victory, taking 3-43. Fittingly, that last match was at Lord's, where Titmus played 358 matches and ensnared 1,198 of his 2,830 first-class victims.

Fred Titmus on Lord's:
"I joined the Lord's ground staff at the tender age of 16 in April 1949 and from then on I never lost sight of the fact that this was the place to be. Lord's – the most fantastic cricket ground in the world, full of history, the home of cricket, set in leafy splendour in my home city of London.

After 60 years of being associated with Lord's I've never lost my love for and admiration of its wonderful atmosphere. Over the years the facilities have improved beyond compare, but its heart and soul are unchanged. I thank my lucky stars that I was able to play the majority of my cricket at such a ground."

FAMOUS PLAYERS

Denis Compton

Denis Compton (1918-1997) first came into the Middlesex side as an 18-year-old in 1936 and immediately shone, becoming the youngest player to reach 1,000 runs in his debut season. The following year he scored 1,980 runs, and his prolific form was rewarded with a Test debut against New Zealand: he scored 65 before being run out. On his debut against Australia in 1938 at Trent Bridge he made 102: he remains England's youngest Test centurion. However, it was in 1947 that Compton enjoyed perhaps the most glorious season any player has experienced. None has approached the 3,816 runs (at an average of 90), all scored at a fair lick, or the 18 centuries he made that season. He also took 73 wickets with his left-arm spin. Unfortunately, persistent knee trouble blighted his career although he enjoyed some exceptional moments, including his highest Test score of 278 against Pakistan at Trent Bridge in 1954. He scored over 5,800 runs in 78 Tests at an average of 50.06; in all first-class cricket he made 38,942 runs (av 51.85) with 123 hundreds, 48 of them scored at his beloved Lord's; he also picked up 622 wickets with his slow left-armers. More than his figures, however, Compton is remembered for his inventive and daring batting and devil-may-care approach to life. His elder brother Leslie, the Middlesex wicket-keeper, was Denis's footballing team-mate at Arsenal: both of them won a League Championship and FA Cup-winner's medal for the north London club.

Colin Bland

Born in Rhodesia in 1938, Colin Bland was one of the most brilliant cover fielders of all time, blessed with great athleticism and a reliable arm honed by hours of practice trying to throw down a single stump. As well as being a wonderful fieldsman, Bland was a very fine batsman, who averaged 49.08 in his 21 Tests for South Africa and made 572 runs (av 71.50) in the home Test series against England in 1964-65. Bland's Test career ended sadly when he injured his knee fielding in a Test Match against Australia in 1966.

Colin Bland on Lord's:

"The first impression one gets when walking or driving through the Grace Gate is the tradition (even when I played): the old Members' Stand, the old press box in the Warner Stand and the feeling of the privilege of playing at the home of cricket. And then there is the atmosphere that cloaks the whole ground, especially when the stands are full. The slope of the ground has brought some adverse comments from players. I heard that one South African player when seeing the ground for the first time remarked that it was a terrible surface. He didn't score a run in either innings. I have reasonably pleasant memories of my appearances at Lord's, the most memorable being my two run-outs of Barrington and Parks, which probably prevented England from scoring a huge total and putting South Africa out of the game. But success or failure during the game never reduces the great experience or pleasure of playing there. Over the last 10 years I have been involved in the coaching courses at the indoor school. They have been good years during which some promising youngsters have attended. It is a superb set-up, well run by Clive Radley. Continued development of the ground, spectator facilities and the Media Centre have enhanced, not spoiled, the excitement everyone enjoys when attending a Test Match at Lord's."

Angus Fraser

Angus Fraser (born 1965) was for a time England's most dependable bowler and would have played more Tests but for injury. He landed the ball on a metaphorical sixpence and invariably looked as tired at the start of a spell as at the end. His 46 Tests yielded 177 wickets at an average of 27.32. Fraser made his Test debut in 1989. Two of his most notable performances came on tour in the West Indies: during the 1993-94 tour he took 8-75 in the Barbados Test Match, and four years later he took 8-53 at Port of Spain (his career-best first-class figures). As a batsman, he was defensive and doughty and helped with some rearguard actions, notably when he and Robert Croft shared a last-wicket stand to save the Old Trafford Test against South Africa in 1998. Fraser was a loyal servant for Middlesex between 1984 and 2002, and captained the county

in the last two seasons of his career. In 290 first-class matches he claimed 886 wickets. After working as cricket correspondent of *The Independent*, he returned to Middlesex as Director of Cricket in January 2009.

Angus Fraser on Lord's:

"I remember attending the ground as a child and even recall entering the pavilion for the first time, when I was smuggled in. I first played at Lord's for Middlesex in 1985 (my debut was a B&H Cup game against Surrey) and continued until 2002. Every game there was a privilege, especially the Test Matches for England. In my first Test there, I bagged eight wickets (including five in an innings) against India in 1990. As a result of my fiver-for, it was great to get on the honours board, a feat I repeated against the West Indies in 1995. Lord's has a special atmosphere. The walk from the dressing room through the Long Room out to the middle is one that all the greats have made. Lord's has changed a lot since I first played there in 1984 and every change to the stands and structures has improved it."

Andrew Strauss

Rarely have players taken to Test cricket as easily as Andrew Strauss. Born in 1977, and making his debut against New Zealand at Lord's in 2004, at the relatively late age of 27, Strauss hit a century in his first Test innings and could have repeated the feat in the second but Nasser Hussain ran him out when he had made 83. He also scored a century in his first overseas Test, against South Africa in December 2004.

A fluent left-hander and reliable slip-fielder, Strauss contributed two centuries to England's 2005 Ashes victory over Australia. A run of poor form in 2007 led to him missing Test Matches, but he re-established himself the following year and, after Kevin Pietersen's resignation, was appointed England captain in January 2009. During the 2008–09 winter Strauss scored five Test centuries, two of them in one Test against India. Although his appearances for the county have been limited by his international commitments, Strauss has been a Middlesex stalwart since making his debut in 1998.

Andrew Strauss on Lord's:

"I have been fortunate enough to spend most of my career playing at Lord's, first for Middlesex and more recently for England. It would be easy for the ground's unique charms to start wearing off but that has certainly not happened. It is without doubt the venue by which all others are measured. A fantastic wicket, excellent practice facilities, the signature slope on the outfield, the distinctive pavilion, and the iconic Media Centre all combine to make this ground the 'home' of cricket. If you add that some of my most memorable innings have been played there, including a century on Test debut on the ground, it is easy to see why it is without doubt my favourite ground in the world, a sentiment that is echoed by the vast majority of cricketers that I have played with or against."

OTHER GROUNDS

John Walker's Ground, Southgate *above*

Southgate Cricket Club was founded in 1855 by John Walker, a member of the well-known family who were key figures in the foundation of Middlesex. Many of the matches played there in the late 19th century attracted 10,000 spectators. While it was initially known as Chapel Fields, it was renamed the Walker Stadium in 1907. Middlesex did not use it as a second ground until 1991, when they returned there to play some one-day matches. Mike Gatting hit one of his highest scores at the ground, making 241 against Essex in his last season, 1998, and sharing an opening stand of 372 with Justin Langer, a Middlesex record for the first wicket.

Uxbridge Cricket Club Ground

The Uxbridge Cricket Club was founded in 1789, and played at various locations in the area before settling at Cricketfield Road in 1858, where it remained until 1970. The club sold the site and acquired a new site nearby at Gatting Way (named after the former Middlesex captain) just opposite Oxbridge Common. The 1997 season saw a remarkable bowling performance at the ground from Lancashire's Peter Martin, who returned match figures of 13-79. Uxbridge now stages county Twenty20 games.

Old Deer Park, Richmond

Cricket has been played at Richmond since 1666. The beautiful ground is located in Old Deer Park on the south bank of the Thames. In 1862, two hundred years after the first games of cricket were played there, Richmond Cricket Club was formed. Geographically in Surrey, the club plays in the Middlesex Cricket League and since 2000 the ground has been occasionally used by Middlesex CCC to stage first and second team matches. The ground is also home to London Welsh Rugby Club.

Allan Lamb

Though born in South Africa in 1954, Allan Lamb took advantage of the fact that his parents had been born in England to play Test cricket for England. From his debut in 1982, he became a fixture in the England middle-order. Famed for his powerful square cut, in 79 Tests he scored 4,656 runs (av 36.09). He was particularly effective against the formidable West Indian bowling quartet of the time, remarkably scoring three centuries in 1984, in a series England lost 5-0. He became an important figure for Northants and captain of the county. In an exceptionally good season in 1995, the club finished runners-up to Warwickshire in the Championship under Lamb's inspirational leadership. In all first-class cricket Lamb scored 32,502 runs (av 48.97), and 89 centuries.

Allan Lamb on the County Ground:

"I played all of my home cricket at Wantage Road. It may not have been the most fashionable ground, but we had some great victories there. In the 1995 season, we won most of our games at home. Many of them were tight games in which I gambled to win. It was a memorable season for supporters and spectators. Now with the ground's improvements it is an enhanced ground on which to play and watch cricket."

NORTHAMPTONSHIRE

While Northants have never won the County Championship, they have finished second on four occasions and won a number of one-day titles. The club was officially formed in July 1878 from an embryonic organisation which is believed to date from 1820 (if this is the case, Northants may well be the oldest of all the counties). After some success in Minor Counties cricket, they were admitted to the County Championship in 1905. The club's first match in the Championship was against Hampshire at Southampton in May 1905.

Northants have never managed to win the Championship, but they have finished runners-up on four occasions. The first of these was in 1912 (when the county finished second to Yorkshire, losing only one of their 18 matches) but unfortunately for the county's supporters, this was not a prelude to a successful era. On the contrary, the inter-War years were notable for a remarkable stretch of 99 matches without winning a single Championship match between May 1935 and May 1939. Between 1919 and 1948, the county failed to finish in the top ten of the table, finishing bottom in 10 of these seasons.

Performances picked up after 1945, especially under the captaincy of Freddie Brown. Another sign of the county's upward fortunes was the selection of Frank Tyson and Keith Andrew for the Ashes-winning MCC tour of Australia in 1954-55. The captaincy passed from Brown to Dennis Brookes, then to Raman Subba Row in 1958. Northants finished runners-up in 1957, 1965 and 1976 and enjoyed success in the one-day competitions, winning knock-out trophies in 1976, 1980 and 1992. Indeed

1976 was probably the county's most successful season ever, as they beat Lancashire in the final of the Gillette Cup and finished runners-up to Middlesex in the Championship.

The county has been served by some top-quality players, including such England stalwarts as the fast bowler Frank Tyson, batsmen Raman Subba Row (who scored the first triple-century for the club) and Allan Lamb, as well as modern-day spin bowler Monty Panesar. The county has also had a number of overseas star players in the past 30 years, notably Bishen Bedi, Kapil Dev, Curtly Ambrose, Anil Kumble and Matthew Hayden.

The County Ground, Northampton

Northants played at the Racecourse Ground in Northampton before their move to the County Ground in 1886. The land was bought for £2,000 and the move was given long-term financial backing by Alfred Cockerill. After hosting Minor Counties cricket, the ground finally hosted its first first-class match in June 1905, with Leicestershire the opponents. As well as cricket, the ground also accommodated a range of sports including cycling, tennis, athletics, bowls and football. It was the home of Northampton Town FC from 1897 until 1994, when they moved to a purpose-built stadium two miles away.

Since 1990 the ground has benefited from a series of improvements. The pavilion was refurbished in 1990-91 and named the Spencer Pavilion, after Earl Spencer (the Spencers are a prominent local family and the current Earl Spencer, brother of the late Princess of Wales, has a cricket pitch on his estate at Althorp). Its seating capacity was increased by an investment of £100,000 in 1996-97. New entrance gates were constructed in 1992-93 and 1997 at the Wantage Road and Abington Avenue

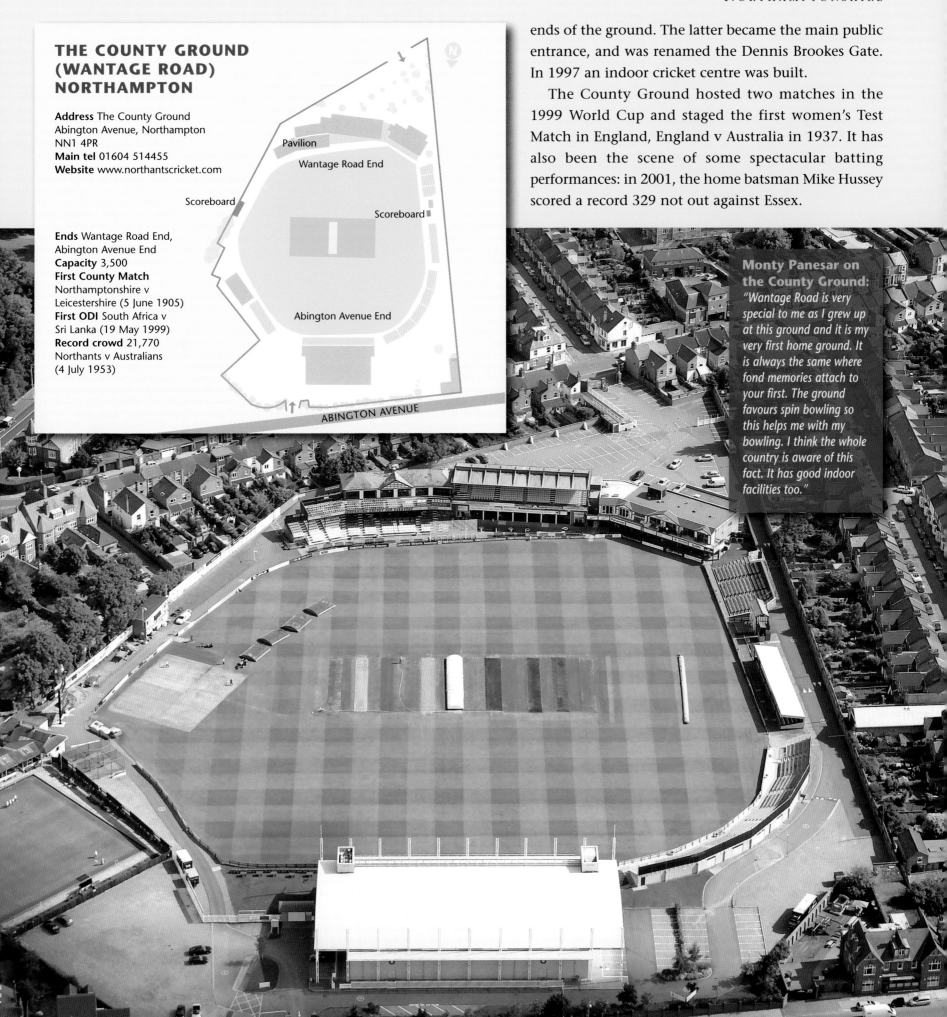

THE COUNTY GROUND (WANTAGE ROAD) NORTHAMPTON

Address The County Ground
Abington Avenue, Northampton
NN1 4PR
Main tel 01604 514455
Website www.northantscricket.com

Ends Wantage Road End,
Abington Avenue End
Capacity 3,500
First County Match
Northamptonshire v
Leicestershire (5 June 1905)
First ODI South Africa v
Sri Lanka (19 May 1999)
Record crowd 21,770
Northants v Australians
(4 July 1953)

Pavilion

Wantage Road End

Scoreboard

Scoreboard

Abington Avenue End

ABINGTON AVENUE

ends of the ground. The latter became the main public entrance, and was renamed the Dennis Brookes Gate. In 1997 an indoor cricket centre was built.

The County Ground hosted two matches in the 1999 World Cup and staged the first women's Test Match in England, England v Australia in 1937. It has also been the scene of some spectacular batting performances: in 2001, the home batsman Mike Hussey scored a record 329 not out against Essex.

Monty Panesar on the County Ground:
"Wantage Road is very special to me as I grew up at this ground and it is my very first home ground. It is always the same where fond memories attach to your first. The ground favours spin bowling so this helps me with my bowling. I think the whole country is aware of this fact. It has good indoor facilities too."

Cyril Perkins

Perkins was a slow left-arm bowler who played 56 matches for Northants between 1934 and 1937, in an era when the side was struggling. In those matches he took 93 wickets at an average of 35.58, with best figures of 6-54. Born in 1911, Cyril Perkins is thought to be the oldest surviving county cricketer and holds the record for playing the most first-class matches without ever being on the winning side. Between 1939 and 1967 Perkins played with considerable success for Suffolk, taking a county record 779 wickets. In 2000 he was included in the Minor Counties Team of the Century.

Cyril Perkins on the County Ground:

"When I played at the County Ground in the 1930s one end was the football ground. The pitch was a bit slow. Once we played Warwickshire, the wicket was dead, the cricket was dull and the crowd got agitated. RES Wyatt, who was not known for his fast scoring, was batting, and the crowd barracked him. He sat down and wouldn't play on until they were quiet. They got the

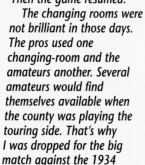

Northants President out, and he spoke to the crowd and told them to be quiet. Then the game resumed.

The changing rooms were not brilliant in those days. The pros used one changing-room and the amateurs another. Several amateurs would find themselves available when the county was playing the touring side. That's why I was dropped for the big match against the 1934 Australians. To the best of my recollection we were paid £5 for a home match and £7 for an away match, as we had to pay our own expenses.

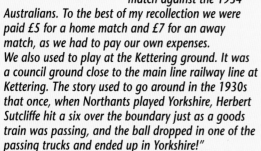

We also used to play at the Kettering ground. It was a council ground close to the main line railway line at Kettering. The story used to go around in the 1930s that once, when Northants played Yorkshire, Herbert Sutcliffe hit a six over the boundary just as a goods train was passing, and the ball dropped in one of the passing trucks and ended up in Yorkshire!"

Frank Tyson

Born in Lancashire in 1930, Frank Tyson obtained residential qualifications to play for Northants, and ended up with 766 first-class wickets. Rated by some as the fastest bowler ever, Tyson took 76 wickets for England in 17 Test Matches at an exceptional average of 18.56. His performances earned him the nickname "Typhoon Tyson", and helped England to retain the Ashes in 1954-55 after beating the Australians (the *pièce de résistance* was his spell of 7-27 during the third Test at Melbourne). On that tour he forged an effective

and potent bowling partnership with Brian Statham. He was a mainstay of the Northants team of the era, contributing to its second place finish in 1957, but after a series of injuries retired early from the game aged 30.

Frank Tyson on the County Ground:

"When I returned from England's Ashes-winning tour in April 1955, my skipper, Len Hutton, gave me one piece of very sound advice: 'If you want to be bowling for England in five years time, Frank,' he said, 'get away from the Northamptonshire pitch.' This opinion of the notoriously slow wicket and the effect that it would have on the fastest bowler in the country was later substantiated by interference by the Midland county's selectors, who consistently chose three left-handed orthodox spinners and only one medium-paced all-rounder – ostensibly to 'take the shine off the ball'. Even when an extra quickie like Surrey's Harry Kelleher slipped under the committee's guard, he was allocated no more than a match ration of 3 or 4 overs from the spinners' match-winning quota of 20! Even the outfield could not escape the Wantage Road stigma; the winter tenants of the northern field were the Northampton soccer team, the depredations of whose boots made out-fielding a bruising experience. Wicket-keeping was pure guesswork as to whether the ball would roll along the ground or hop into the fielder's forearms. Thankfully 'the old order changeth'. The Cobblers soccer side have moved out and cricket monopolises all of the Cockerill Trust ground. Modern office, changing and catering facilities have mushroomed around the oval. The pitch is now more of a placid batting surface than a raging turner. It is the home of 400-run totals and batsmen's innings of 300. It oozes huge totals in August."

David Capel

As a talented all-rounder, David Capel, born in 1963, was given the unenviable task of being the next Ian Botham. He played for Northants from 1981 to 1998 and was part of teams which won one-day titles for the county. In 313 first-class matches he scored 12,202 runs and took 546 wickets. He made his Test debut in 1987 and was to play 15 Tests over the next three years. He struggled to make his mark at Test level, although he did have the distinction of dismissing Viv Richards three times. He was appointed head coach in 2006.

David Capel on the County Ground:

"Playing cricket at the County Ground, Northampton, during the 1980s and 1990s as a

local Northampton player was always special for me. In those days it was not the most scenic ground nor could it be said that the pitch or the facilities were favourable in comparison to other grounds around England, but it holds a special place in my memory for the great matches we played in the past as well as the warmth of the people. With it being home for me it holds memories of the special players that played there and of my friends, mentors and coaches with whom I spent so many happy days, playing, socialising and sharing our lives. The ground has improved greatly over the past decade and there are grand plans for further improvements in the near future."

David Sales

Born in 1977, Sales made an immediate impression scoring 210 not out as a precocious 18-year-old for Northants against Worcestershire in 1996. He developed into a consistent scorer, culminating in a prolific season in 1999, when he scored 1,291 runs at an average of over 50. During that season he made 303 not out against Essex at Northampton, thereby becoming the youngest Englishman to make a triple century. He was made Northants captain in 2004.

David Sales on the County Ground:

"It's a joy to play at the County Ground with its intimate atmosphere. The ground has changed over the years for the better and the pitch has always been a favourite of mine. With so many big names having played here, it has always been a focus for the local sporting community."

Monty Panesar

Following his Test debut in March 2006 against India, Monty Panesar (born 1982) has made his mark on the international scene with over 100 Test

wickets to his name. Born to Indian Punjabi parents, he wears a distinctive black head-dress and is the first Sikh to play for England. The left-arm spinner has become a popular figure with England's supporters and is a proud product of Northants, for whom he has played since 2001.

OTHER GROUNDS

Wardown Park, Luton *above & left*

Northants first played at Wardown Park in Luton in 1986, and continued playing there until their last county game against Gloucestershire in 1997. The ground is now used by Minor Counties side Bedfordshire.

Campbell Park, Milton Keynes *(not pictured)*

This ground is located in the middle of a park, close to central Milton Keynes. It was constructed in 1990 and the first full season of cricket was in 1996. Northants' first fixture was a one-day match against Nottinghamshire on 8 June 1997. It has a capacity of 7,500 and has been used in recent seasons for Twenty20 matches.

NOTTINGHAMSHIRE

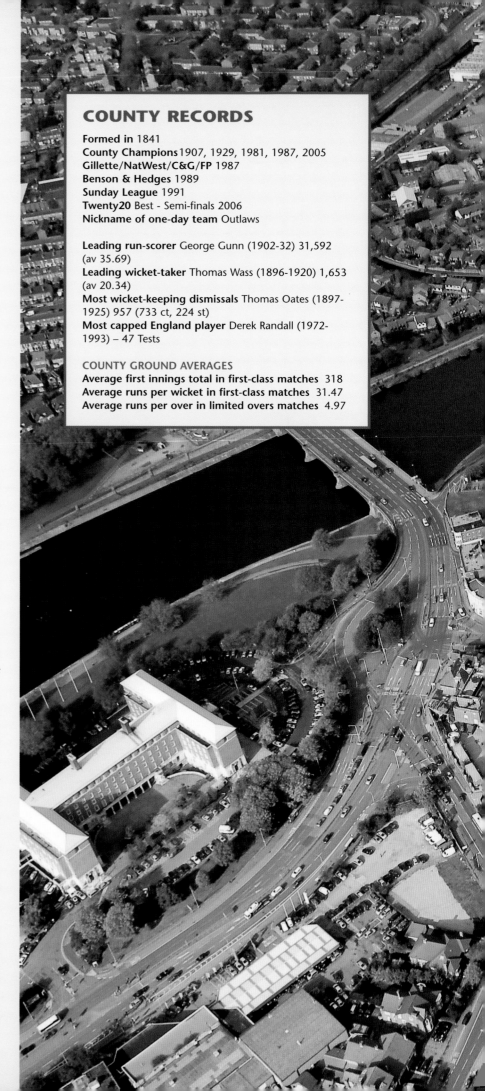

Cricket has deep roots in Nottinghamshire, with Trent Bridge having hosted county cricket since 1840. Nottinghamshire, commonly refered to as "Notts", won the Championship four times in the 20th century and again in 2005.

Nottinghamshire CCC was formally constituted in 1841, although there had been a skeleton Notts team that had started playing matches against other counties in 1835. After its foundation, Notts became a significant force in the game, first becoming champion county in 1852 (shared with Sussex) and emerging as the best team in the country in the 1860s and 1870s. Deftly led by George Parr and Richard Daft, Notts had by 1890 won the unofficial championship 18 times.

Nottinghamshire entered the official Championship in 1890, and first won the competition outright in the 1907 season. That season, the brothers George and John Gunn were mainstays of the batting, whilst the most penetrative bowlers were the spinners Albert Hallam and Thomas Wass. The idiosyncratic George Gunn continued to appear for Notts until the ripe old age of 53 – playing the last of his 15 Test Matches when he was almost 51 – and remains the only man to exceed 30,000 runs for the county. Playing for Notts against Warwickshire in 1931, the penultimate year of his career, George (183) and his son GV Gunn (100 not out) provided the only instance in first-class cricket of a father and son scoring a century in the same innings.

Under the inspirational leadership of Arthur Carr, Notts were one of the best sides in the Championship, finishing second in 1922, 1923 and 1927 and winning the Champion-ship in 1929. An important element of their success was the opening attack of Harold Larwood and Bill Voce, who went on to spearhead the England bowling in the "Bodyline" series. Larwood, who had already played a part in England's Ashes

Reg Simpson on Trent Bridge:
"Having played at Trent Bridge for 17 years my memories are far too numerous to enumerate. I will refer to one or two briefly. My first 100 in first-class cricket was particularly outstanding as it turned into a double century. Obviously I scored many more, including the first to be scored by a Notts batsman in a Test Match at Trent Bridge. During my nine years as captain, one outstanding memory was bowling underarm to Wilf Wooller, the Glamorgan captain, after which wickets fell rapidly."

TRENT BRIDGE, NOTTINGHAM

Address Trent Bridge,
Nottingham NG2 6AG
Main tel 0115 982 3000
Website www.trentbridge.co.uk

Ends Pavilion End, Radcliffe Road End
First County Match
Nottinghamshire
v Sussex (27 July 1840)
First Test Match England
v Australia (1 June 1899)
First ODI England v Pakistan
(31 August 1974)
Capacity 17,000
Record crowd 35,000
Nottinghamshire v Surrey
(15 May 1948)

Tim Robinson on Trent Bridge:
"As a local lad, I was thrilled to make my Trent Bridge debut in 1978. It was always the Mecca of cricket locally. Not long after, we sealed the Championship at the ground in the 1981 season, with victory over Glamorgan. Over the years Chris Broad and I enjoyed many good opening partnerships at the ground. We would thrive off each other. A particular thrill was playing for England at my home ground, especially against Australia in 1985. The stadium has changed in recent years, but even with all the new stands and modern facilities, it has a homely and friendly atmosphere."

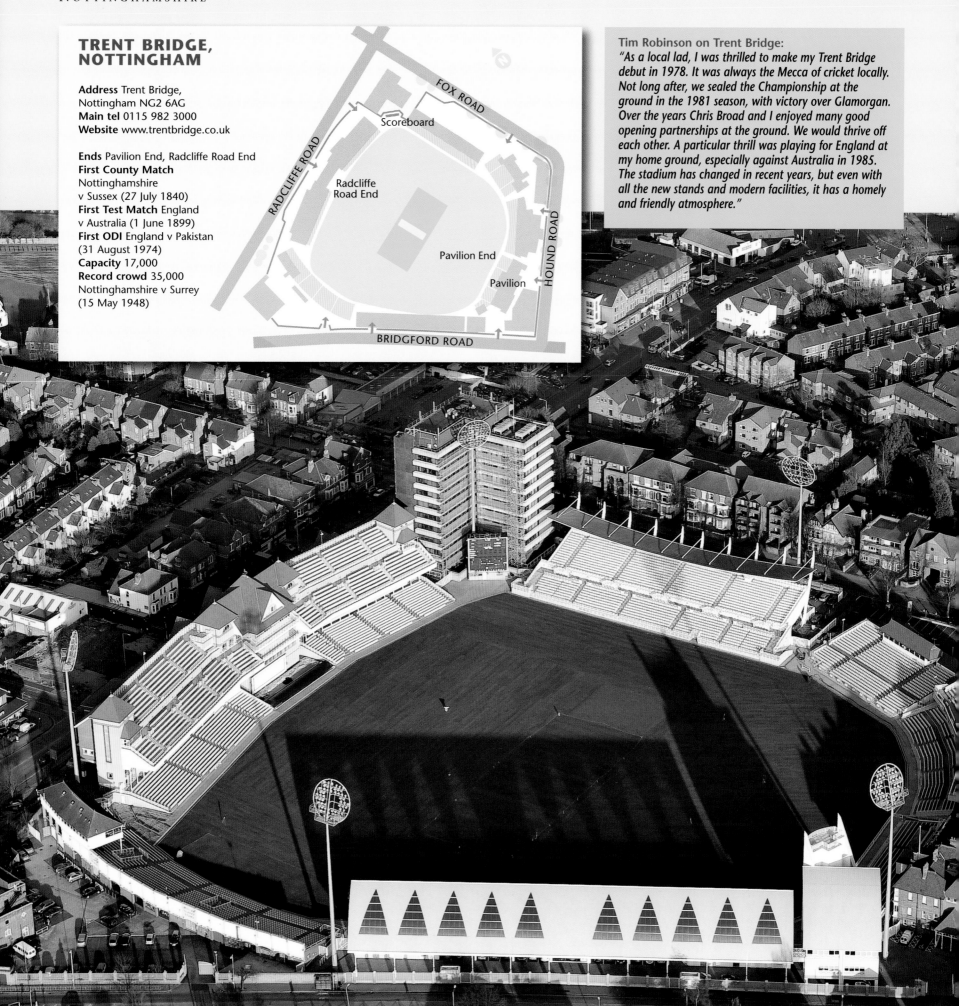

triumph in 1926, took 100 wickets in county cricket at an average of 17 the following season and was to remain a major weapon in the Notts attack until 1938.

After the Second World War, Joe Hardstaff and Reg Simpson stood out as elegant batsmen, and the latter took over the captaincy in 1951, in what was a difficult period for the county, characterised by inconsistent performances.

Spirits were lifted by the signing of the Australian leg-spin bowler Bruce Dooland in 1952, following lamentable performances in the Championships in both 1951 and 1952; in five seasons, Dooland took 808 wickets, but left in 1957 to return to Australia.

While another top overseas player arrived in the form of Garry Sobers (left) in 1968 (who in one match for the county hit six sixes in an over against Glamorgan), further success proved elusive until the 1980s. It was then that top overseas players, such as the South African Clive Rice (who joined in 1975) and the New Zealand all-rounder Richard Hadlee, joined forces with English talent such as Derek Randall and Tim Robinson, to restore glory to the Trent Bridge side. Championships were won in 1981 and 1987, and a further two one-day trophies were secured in this decade.

Despite some up and down performances in recent times, Nottinghamshire won the Championship again in 2005 under the leadership of another overseas player, the experienced New Zealand batsman Stephen Fleming.

Trent Bridge, Nottingham

The history of Trent Bridge goes back to William Clarke, the main organiser of the embryonic Nottinghamshire team in the 1830s. After he married Mrs Chapman, the landlady at the Trent Bridge Inn in 1837, the team started playing matches on a ground outside the inn. The Trent Bridge ground evolved from this, with the first inter-county match being played against Sussex in 1840. The ground was also used by the local football side Notts County (the oldest Football League club, formed in 1862) until 1910.

The first Test Match played at Trent Bridge took place in 1899 against Australia (it was the second oldest ground in England to hold a Test after Lord's and the third oldest in the world). The ground stayed in the Clarke family's hands until 1919, when the club purchased it (though a 99-year lease had been signed in 1899).

Parts of the ground are very old – the pavilion was originally designed by HM Townsend and built in 1886 – though it was added to over the course of the 20th century. A famous tree stood behind the Parr Stand, until it was blown down by a gale in 1976; the tree was named after the big-striking batsman George Parr, who famously hit it when playing for the county between 1845 and 1870. Harold Larwood and Bill Voce also have a stand named after them.

In 1990 the William Clarke Stand was built, while the Radcliffe Road Stand was completed in 1998 at a cost of £7.2m and includes a cricket centre. A further £1.9m was spent on the Fox Road stand, which opened in 2002; another redevelopment, costing £8.2m, was completed in 2008.

Test Matches

Following its first Test in 1899, Trent Bridge has hosted many notable and exciting Test Matches. Superb batting performances include Denis Compton's 278 against Pakistan in 1954, Tom Graveney's 258 against the West Indies in 1958 and Viv Richards' 232 for the West Indies in 1976. In the 1989 Ashes Test, the Australian opening pair Mark Taylor and Geoff Marsh batted brilliantly, reaching 301 without loss at the end of the first day's play and ended up putting on 329 for the first wicket, the record opening stand in Ashes history. Another Australian batsman, Charlie Macartney, scored a triple century against Notts off 221 balls in 205 minutes in 1921 – the second fastest triple hundred ever; his 345 remains the highest score at the ground.

Sir Richard Hadlee

Sir Richard Hadlee (born 1951) made his Test debut in 1973 and by the time his Test career drew to a close in 1990, he had built a reputation as the greatest all-rounder to have come out of New Zealand. In 86 Test Matches he took 431 wickets at an average of 22.29 and scored 3,124 runs (av 27.16). He was the first bowler to pass the 400 wicket mark in Test cricket. Hadlee reserved some of his special performances for Tests in England. His 200th Test wicket came in a Test against England at Trent Bridge in 1983 whilst also at his adopted home ground three years later he led New Zealand to victory against England grabbing 10 wickets and scoring 68 in the first innings (the series finished 1-0 to the visitors). His final Test Match was played at Edgbaston in 1990 and he fittingly took five wickets, one of them with his very last ball in Test cricket. For Notts between 1978 and 1987 he was a brilliant performer. Though Test call-ups and injuries meant he played only three full seasons at Trent Bridge, as a measure of his success, in those seasons he took 105 wickets (1981), 117 wickets (1984) and 97 wickets (1987) at averages of below 15 each time. In the latter two seasons he also exceeded 1,000 runs, in 1984 becoming the first man to do the double since Fred Titmus 17 years earlier. Only another Notts all-rounder Franklin Stephenson, in 1988, has since repeated the feat. Hadlee's brilliant all-round play was a key factor in Notts' resurgence and success in the 1980s. His career record at Trent Bridge is exceptional: he scored 2,746 runs (av 35.66) and took 375 wickets at the remarkably low average of 13.86. As well as Notts, he also played club cricket for Canterbury and Tasmania. In 1990 he was knighted for services to cricket. Latterly he became a media commentator and the chairman of the New Zealand Cricket Board.

Sir Richard Hadlee on Trent Bridge:

"Trent Bridge is a special ground and holds many memories for me. I played for Nottinghamshire for 10 years as a professional: that experience fine-tuned me as a player and made me the player I turned out to be. During that time we won two County Championships – in 1981 and 1987. On both occasions the last game of the season was against Glamorgan at home – matches we had to win and did. There were wonderful scenes of jubilation and emotion. Notts had earned considerable respect during that era – something that had been missing for many years.

In 1984 I became the first player for 17 years to achieve the coveted double. The 1,000th run was scored off the bowling of Chris Old at Trent Bridge (the 100th wicket had been achieved a week earlier at Blackpool). Mission accomplished! It was a great delight for me and some relief as I had attempted this feat on two previous occasions.

In 1973 I played my first Test Match in England at Trent Bridge. We lost the match, and I captured only one wicket, but New Zealand nearly pulled off a remarkable victory – set 479 to win we were only 39 runs short. However, in 1986 we defeated England at Trent Bridge and went on to achieve our first ever series win in England. I was named Man of the Match, capturing 10 wickets and scoring 68.

In the 1980s bowler friendly pitches (grassy wickets) were produced at Trent Bridge to ensure results – it was fair for all sides who invariably had quality pace attacks who could utilise conditions. Notts bowlers generally bowled a fuller length and were better rewarded. The Test pitches were white in colour and bowlers had to work harder for their successes.

The Trent Bridge crowds were always supportive and appreciated good cricket. Club supporters and members treated me favourably when I was playing for New Zealand.

Architecturally, the ground has well and truly changed today, but the façade of the old pavilion remains. There is still plenty of tradition and history with old photos, memorabilia and magic moments on display reflecting a great club and cricket ground. I donated a limited edition print of my bowling action titled 'The Challenge' thanking the club for the 10 wonderful years they supported me during my time as a professional player – this print is on display in a prominent position as the players come down the stairs from their dressing room. The old Radcliffe Road Stand has now been replaced with the new and imposing stand. The old stand had plenty of noise and atmosphere from supporters. I could actually see many familiar faces sitting in the seats day after day watching county games."

Harold Larwood

Harold Larwood (1904-1995) left school at 14 to work in the coalmines but, owing to a precocious talent, made his Notts debut as a 19-year-old in 1924. His first England appearance soon followed in 1926 and as a ferocious fast bowler, he helped his country to reclaim the Ashes that year. Larwood continued to develop as a world-class bowler. He became famous for the part he played in the 1932-33 "Bodyline" series when the England team led by Douglas Jardine adopted the "Leg Theory" and won the Ashes, if few friends in the cricketing world; in what was his last Test series Larwood took 33 wickets (av 19.51) as well as scoring 98 – then the highest score by a nightwatchman – in his last Test innings. Larwood played for

Notts until 1938 and in 361 first-class matches claimed 1,427 wickets at the impressive average of 17.51. Five times – 1927, 1928, 1931, 1932 and 1936 – he headed the English first-class bowling averages.

Reg Simpson

Reg Simpson (born 1920) was an elegant opening batsman who played 27 Test Matches for England. The start of his career was delayed by the Second World War (he first played for Sind in India where he was stationed with the RAF), and he made his Notts debut in 1946. The runs flowed from his bat and in 495 first-class matches he amassed 30,546 runs including 64 centuries. He became Notts captain in 1951 and was an enterprising leader on the field until 1960, retiring three years later. His England debut came in 1948 against South Africa; the most memorable of his four Test centuries – two of them at Trent Bridge – was the 156 not out he scored against Australia in 1950-51, which enabled England to win the fifth Test at Melbourne after a rampant Australia had won the first four of the series – England's first victory in an Ashes Test since 1938. Simpson made nine double centuries for the county, but his highest score – 259 – was made for the MCC against New South Wales in 1950-51. After retiring from playing, he became managing director of the Notts bat-makers Gunn & Moore.

William "Dusty" Hare

Hare, born in Newark in 1952, was a famous rugby player, but also enjoyed a brief county cricket career with Nottinghamshire. A full-back, he represented Nottingham RFC and Leicester Tigers and scored more points in his career – 7,337 – than anyone else in professional rugby. In his youth, Hare was a promising batsman and played 10 first-class matches between 1971 and 1977. He started playing for the Second XI in 1969 and later captained the team.

"Dusty" Hare on Trent Bridge:

"I've always thought Trent Bridge to be the nicest of the Test grounds. Its a very pretty ground and support for Test Matches was always very good. It's a historic ground and it meant so much to me to go there. As a Newark-born lad, I was a Notts supporter and I was always thrilled to watch a match at the ground. I first went there as a spectator as a young lad, and saw the South African Graeme Pollock score 125 in the second Test Match of the 1965 series in front of a full house. I left school to be a cricketer, but my rugby game improved, while my cricket stayed the same. I played for Notts as a batsman from 1971 to 1977. I wish I had been a better player. In all, I played 10 first-class games and was captain of the second team for a while. For the firsts my top score was 36, with an average of 12. Highlights at Trent Bridge included beating Sussex in a Gillette Cup match. Against Middlesex in the John Player League, owing to freak circumstances, I had to take over as wicket-keeper; our regular 'keeper Basher Hassan broke his thumb while batting so I took the gloves and managed to stump Mike Brearley!"

Tim Robinson

Tim Robinson (born 1958) was a methodical opening batsman who played for Nottinghamshire between 1978 and 1999. He formed a fruitful opening partnership with the more free-flowing left-hander Chris Broad after the latter joined from Gloucestershire in 1984. Robinson was the Notts captain from 1988 to 1995 and scored a total of 27,571 runs (av 42.63) and 63 hundreds in 425 first-class matches – he was Notts' second highest run-scorer of all time. Robinson enjoyed a particularly successful summer with the bat in 1984, scoring 2,032 runs at an average of 50.80, which led him to the international stage. The highlights of his 29 Tests as an England player were 160 in only his second Test against India in 1984-85 and two big centuries – 175 and 148, in the latter innings sharing a second wicket partnership of 331 with David Gower – against the Australians in the Ashes contest in the summer of 1985; he played his last Test also against Australia in 1989. Robinson has been a first-class umpire since 2007.

Paul Johnson

A one-club man, Paul Johnson (born 1965) joined Notts as a 16-year-old and played for the county from 1982 to 2002. He was an extremely prolific county batsman, amassing over 20,000 runs in 371 first-class matches (this puts him in the top 10 Notts run-scorers of all time). He passed 1,000 runs for the season on nine occasions. He was also a brilliant one-day player, becoming the highest run-scorer for Notts in the Sunday League in 2001. His highest one-day innings was 167 not out against Kent at Trent Bridge in 1993, which remains Notts' highest score in the Sunday League. Johnson was Notts captain from 1996 to 1998, and

retired in 2002, subsequently becoming a coach at Trent Bridge.

Paul Johnson on Trent Bridge:

"For me, the intimacy of Trent Bridge makes it the best ground in the country and, Lord's aside, no ground comes close to its atmosphere. Even with a small crowd, there is a nice feeling around the ground. I was fortunate to spend my entire career with Notts."

Jason Gallian

Born in Sydney in 1971, Jason Gallian captained Australia in two Under-19 Test matches but after playing for Oxford University, he made his first-class debut for Lancashire in 1990. He played eight seasons for the county (his 312 against Derbyshire in 1996 remains the record for the highest individual score at Old Trafford) before moving to Notts as captain in 1997. By then, he had already played his three Tests for England in 1995, two of which came against the West Indies. Gallian was a lynchpin of the Notts batting and led them to promotion in both the Championship and the Sunday League in 2004. In 2005 he was replaced by Stephen Fleming as captain, but responded well, scoring over 1,000 runs. During that season he performed what *Wisden* described as "an unprecedented and uniquely irritating feat in anyone's career, never mind a single season", of twice being run out for 199! Gallian never went on to score a double century for Notts. In 2008 he moved to Essex and in his first season there passed the landmark of 15,000 runs in first-class cricket.

Jason Gallian on Trent Bridge:

"When I joined Notts in 1997, one of the selling points was the ground at Trent Bridge. It became my home ground for the next 10 years and I soon grew to appreciate its intimacy and family feeling. It also has a great tradition, as one of the oldest Test match venues in the world. In the 2004 and 2005 seasons, we enjoyed some great victories there, which led us to the second division and first division titles in successive seasons. Trent Bridge has always been a pretty ground and, over the past few years, it has had to make some serious developments."

OTHER GROUNDS

Town Ground, Worksop *above*
Nottinghamshire first played at the Town Ground in Worksop in 1921 in a match against Derbyshire. It continued to use the ground for the remainder of the 20th century; the last Championship match played there was in 1998.

Worksop College *right*
Set amidst 650 acres of national parkland on the edge of Sherwood Forest, this elegant ground is part of the independent Worksop College. The ground stages both Second XI Championship and Trophy matches.

SOMERSET

The West Country county was formed in 1875 and enjoyed a golden era in the 1970s and 1980s, reaching its zenith in the 1979 season, when it captured the first trophies in its history with the help of a trio of cricketing greats: Sir Ian Botham, Sir Viv Richards and Joel Garner.

Someset was founded in 1875 following a meeting in Devon and while it played first-class cricket from 1882 to 1886 it fell out of the game's elite for a short period after that. However, its strong performances in Minor Counties cricket led to its re-entry to the top tier in 1891, the year after the official County Championship was established, and it finished third in 1892.

Somerset's performances for most of the 20th century were patchy, though there were some eye-catching feats along the way. For example, in the three seasons between 1900 and 1902 the only two matches that the all-conquering Yorkshire side lost were both to Somerset; despite this, the Taunton-based county finished 11th, 13th and 7th in those seasons. More typical of their form was that they finished bottom of the Championship in four out of seven seasons in the run-up to the First World War.

A key player in this era was Ernie Robson (1895-1923), who took over 1,100 wickets and scored in excess of 12,000 runs. He played till a ripe age, making a hundred after his 50th birthday; the following season, he hit a six in the final over of the game to lead his county to victory over the champions, Middlesex. This period saw the emergence of the slow left-arm bowler Jack White, who played between 1909 to 1937 and took 100 or more wickets each season from 1919 to 1932. One of White's protégés, the spin bowler, Horace Hazell, went on to take 957 wickets in 17 war-interrupted seasons from 1929. The 1930s also saw the

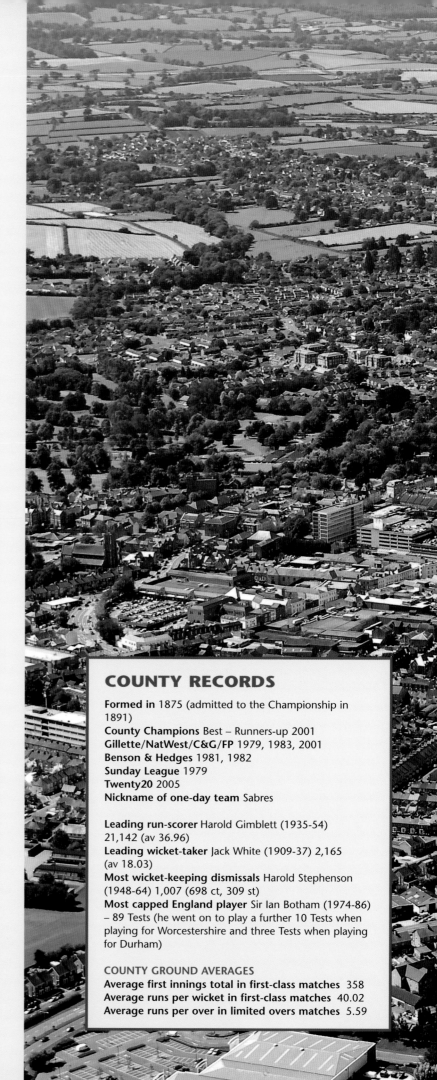

COUNTY RECORDS

Formed in 1875 (admitted to the Championship in 1891)
County Champions Best – Runners-up 2001
Gillette/NatWest/C&G/FP 1979, 1983, 2001
Benson & Hedges 1981, 1982
Sunday League 1979
Twenty20 2005
Nickname of one-day team Sabres

Leading run-scorer Harold Gimblett (1935-54) 21,142 (av 36.96)
Leading wicket-taker Jack White (1909-37) 2,165 (av 18.03)
Most wicket-keeping dismissals Harold Stephenson (1948-64) 1,007 (698 ct, 309 st)
Most capped England player Sir Ian Botham (1974-86) – 89 Tests (he went on to play a further 10 Tests when playing for Worcestershire and three Tests when playing for Durham)

COUNTY GROUND AVERAGES
Average first innings total in first-class matches 358
Average runs per wicket in first-class matches 40.02
Average runs per over in limited overs matches 5.59

Sir Ian Botham

One of the greatest all-rounders of all time, Botham played for Somerset between 1974 and 1986, and built his reputation there – until the county's decision to dispose of the services of Richards and Garner led him to join Worcestershire in 1986. In 172 matches for the county, Botham scored 8,686 runs (av 36.04) and took 489 wickets (av 29.52). He enjoyed batting on home turf, averaging 42.29 at Taunton. Botham was a key part of Somerset's success from 1979 onwards and when Brian Rose was injured, led them to a NatWest Trophy triumph in 1983. The all-rounder enjoyed a remarkable season with the bat in 1985, averaging over 100 in the Championship and hitting a record 80 sixes that season. Despite this, the county floundered – it finished bottom of the table that year. On the international stage, Botham played 102 Tests for England (he was briefly captain for 12 Tests between 1980 and 1981) and took 383 wickets (av 28.40), scored 5,200 runs (av 33.54), and, as a brilliant slip fielder, took 120 catches.

Sir Ian Botham on the County Ground:

"Taunton is where it all started and where I played alongside the likes of Sir Viv Richards, Joel Garner, Brian Rose and Peter Denning. We were a side which won so many trophies, we felt invincible in one-day cricket. I loved playing at Taunton because we intimidated the opposition – it was a compact ground, with 10,000 supporters crammed in there. It felt like the opposition just didn't want to come out of their dressing-room. Somerset CCC was just one happy family. My favourite moment was returning from Lord's with the trophies – we won five trophies in five years and did the double after 103 years of not winning anything."

THE COUNTY GROUND, TAUNTON

River Tone

River End

Pavilion

PRIORY BRIDGE ROAD

Scoreboard

Scoreboard

Address The County Ground
St James's Street, Taunton
Somerset TA1 1JT
Main tel 0845 337 1875
Website www.somersetcountycc.co.uk

Old Pavilion End

Ends River End,
Old Pavilion End
Capacity 7,000 (15,000 with
temporary seating for ODIs)
First County Match Somerset
v Hampshire (8 August 1882)
First ODI England v
Sri Lanka (11 June 1983)
Record crowd 8,450
Sri Lanka v India (26 May 1999)

Old Pavilion

PRIORY AVENUE

rise of perhaps the county's leading home-grown batsman, Harold Gimblett, who scored over 21,000 runs for the county, including 49 hundreds, between 1935 and 1954. His debut, against Essex at Frome in 1935, is the stuff of legends. An emergency last-minute selection, he came in to bat in a crisis – Somerset were 107 for 6 – and scored 123 in 80 minutes.

In the mid-20th century there were some low points. The county finished bottom of the Championship several times, including in four consecutive seasons from 1952.

It was only when the Yorkshireman Brian Close assembled a team with the world-class talents of Ian Botham and the West Indians Viv Richards and Joel Garner that the county became a serious force. Close joined Somerset in 1971 and had a huge influence until his retirement in 1977, as a batsman, a fearless short-leg fielder and an ever-optimistic captain. Never previously having won a trophy, Somerset clinched two competitions in the space of two days in the 1979 season: the Sunday League and the knock-out competition, then known as the Gillette Cup. The team won three further one-day trophies in the next four seasons but was ruptured by the club's decision to dispense with the services of Richards and Garner and instead to choose the New Zealander Martin Crowe as its overseas player for the 1987 season, a decision which led to Botham also leaving the county.

In recent times, Somerset have produced England regulars

Andrew Caddick and Marcus Trescothick. The county almost won its first Championship in 2001, finishing as runners-up, and secured the Twenty20 competition in the 2005 season.

The County Ground, Taunton

Somerset played their first home match at the County Ground in 1882 against Hampshire, and later that season the ground played host to the visiting Australians. Prior to that Somerset led a nomadic existence, playing at a number of grounds, including Fullands School in Taunton.

The County Ground, by the river Tone, was acquired by the county from the Taunton Athletic Company. It hosted its first official Championship match against Lancashire in 1891. Over the intervening years, the ground has seen a number of redevelopments. The greyhound track which encircled it was removed in the 1970s. The pavilion, originally constructed in 1891, was rebuilt in modern times and renamed the Colin Atkinson Pavilion in 1990. Other facilities have been built including the Somerset cricket school and the Ian Botham Stand,

constructed in 1998; the Sir Vivian Richards Gates are at the Priory Bridge Road entrance.

The County Ground was where Sir Jack Hobbs scored a hundred in each innings for Surrey to equal and surpass WG Grace's then record number of centuries. It has also witnessed some sparkling batting performances from leading modern batsmen: in 1985 Viv Richards scored 322 runs in one day against Warwickshire and in 1988 Graeme Hick scored his memorable 405 not out for Worcestershire. In the international game, the ground hosted matches at the 1983 and 1999 World Cups, and in 2006 it became the official home of the English women's cricket team.

The County Ground is currently undergoing a £60m redevelopment, with the aim of completion by 2012. The new Members' Stand and West Stand have already been completed, adding 3,000 more seats to the ground. On the eastern side a new Club Hub is being built, incorporating new changing rooms, gym, office space and restaurants.

Vic Marks on the County Ground:

"I know from personal experience that Taunton can be a bowler's graveyard. In fact deliveries can often end up in the graveyard or in the river at the other end. Yet Taunton is one of the finest county grounds in the country. Spectators can meander in from the town centre and immediately they are intimately involved in the action, so short are the boundaries. From your seat you can spot a bowler's raised eyebrow at an umpire's decision. Over the years Taunton has been graced by some of the greats of the game from every corner of the globe: Gimblett, Alley, Greg Chappell, Viv Richards, Garner, Gavaskar, Botham, Martin Crowe, Steve Waugh, Ponting, Graeme Smith, Caddick, Trescothick and Langer. And they all enjoyed playing there. In 2008 a major overhaul was undertaken to enlarge the capacity and improve facilities. But that wonderful intimacy will remain."

Jack White

A local boy and farmer, Jack White (1891-1961) made his Somerset debut in 1909. In a not particularly successful era for the county, he was a prolific bowler, taking 2,165 wickets in county cricket and becoming the county's leading wicket-taker of all time; he also scored more than 11,000 runs. A very accurate slow left-armer, White was especially effective between 1919 and 1932, when he took over 100 wickets in each season (and in two of them, topped 1,000 runs with the bat). He played 15 Tests for England and his local supporters were particularly delighted when his 25 wickets helped England to reclaim the Ashes in Australia in 1928-29 and celebrated with him on the streets of Somerset. White's best performance for England came in the Adelaide Test of that series when he took 13 wickets. He captained Somerset for five years between 1927 and 1931 and became the county's President in 1960, the year before his death.

Brian Rose

Born in 1950, Brian Rose made his first-class debut in 1969 but it was not until a decade later that he really made his mark. Having succeeded Brian Close as captain for the 1978 season, he led Somerset to success the following year in the Gillette Cup and the Sunday League. By 1983 he had led the county to three further one-day trophies. As a left-handed batsman, he scored 13,236 runs at 33.25

in 270 first-class matches. His successful county captaincy and run-scoring meant he found his way into the England side in 1979. Though he enjoyed a good series against the formidable West Indies fast-bowling attack in 1980, making 243 runs in three Tests, he developed eye trouble which led to his playing the last of his nine Tests in 1981. After retiring in 1987, he returned to his previous job of teaching, but maintained his links with Somerset, becoming chairman and subsequently director of cricket.

Brian Rose on the County Ground:
"We had some glorious years playing at the County Ground from 1978 to 1983. The noise and excitement generated was palpable; at times it was a real cauldron of an atmosphere. One particular game sticks in the memory, a Gillette Cup match in 1978, which we won in a very tight finish. That day I had Botham and Garner bowling at their best and the atmosphere in the ground was very intimidating for the opposing batsmen. If you spoke with any of the international players who played there, they would hold it dear. The atmosphere there is unique amongst English grounds. It is almost similar to Barbados."

Sir Viv Richards

One of the greatest batsmen ever to play the game, Viv Richards (born 1952) had a long association with Somerset, playing for them between 1974 and 1986. He was instrumental in the club's most successful ever era, though things turned sour towards the end when the county performed badly in the 1985 and 1986 seasons, and Richards' contract was controversially not renewed. However he is still remembered at Taunton for his scintillating batting for the county – in a single day's play in 1985 he scored 322 against Warwickshire. Overall in 191 first-class matches for Somerset he scored 14,698 runs at the handsome average of 49.82; he also picked up 96 wickets with shrewd off-spin. He particularly excelled at Taunton,

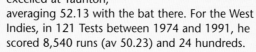

averaging 52.13 with the bat there. For the West Indies, in 121 Tests between 1974 and 1991, he scored 8,540 runs (av 50.23) and 24 hundreds.

Joel Garner

Standing 6ft 8in, "Big Bird" Joel Garner (born 1952) was another key figure in the successful Somerset team from the late 1970s. He first played for the county in 1977 and in his county career took 338 wickets at an average of 18.10. He contributed greatly towards Somerset's one-day success, and bowled the West Indies to World Cup glory in 1979, obtaining the best-ever figures in a World Cup Final of 5-38. Though regarded as particularly lethal as a one-day bowler, he was also a central part of the formidable West Indies side of the 1980s, playing 58 Tests between 1977 and 1987. His 259 Test wickets came at the very economical rate of 20.97.

Vic Marks

Familiar to *Test Match Special* listeners for his characteristic chuckle, Vic Marks (born 1955) is both a radio commentator and a print journalist. As a player, he enjoyed a distinguished career with Somerset, for whom he played between 1975 and 1989 (he also appeared in Western Australia's victorious 1986-87 Sheffield Shield side). With his off-spin and capable batting, Marks was a useful all-round player. In 342 first-class matches he claimed 859 wickets, with best figures of 8-17 for Somerset against Lancashire at Bath in 1985, and

scored 12,419 runs (av 30.29). He was a valuable part of the successful Somerset side from 1979 onwards, and an important character in a team with a number of high-profile stars. He captained the side in 1989. In international cricket, while he played only six Tests, he was an important member of England's one-day team. In total, he played 34 one-day internationals taking 44 wickets at a fine average of 25.79 (including 5-20 against New Zealand in 1984 and another five-wicket haul against Sri Lanka in the 1983 World Cup).

Andy Caddick

Born in Christchurch, New Zealand, in 1968, Andy Caddick made his first-class debut for Somerset in 1991. Making use of his 6ft 5in height, Caddick soon proved a hit on the county circuit. He returned his best figures for the county in the 1993 season, taking 9-32 against Lancashire at Taunton. Having settled in England, he qualified for the national side and made his Test debut in 1993. In 62 Test Matches, he took 234 wickets at just under 30. Highlights included four wickets in a single over against the West Indies in 2000 (the tourists were bowled out for a paltry 61). In his last Test, in Australia in 2002-03, he took 10 wickets. On the county scene, he remained a consistent performer for Somerset, taking his 1,000th first-class wicket during the 2005 season. Whilst his best season was 1998, when he claimed 105 first-class wickets, in 2007 he again finished as the leading English wicket-taker. Caddick spearheaded the attack when Somerset captured the C&G Trophy in 2001and the Twenty20 Cup in 2005, taking 2-21 in the Twenty20 Cup Final against Lancs.

Andy Caddick on the County Ground:
"My first match at Taunton was a trial match against the Australians when I was smashed to all parts of the ground. This was followed by my first-class debut against the West Indians in 1991. My first wicket was Desmond Haynes, caught trying to pull me and I followed this by having Richie Richardson caught at

slip. It was a good wicket then and still is now. It's a true test of bat and ball, with enough bounce to disturb good-quality batsmen, but bowlers have to work for their wickets. Some of my most memorable performances came at Taunton and the 9-32 I took against Lancashire in the 1993 season stands out. In all it's a wonderful ground."

OTHER GROUNDS

The Recreation Ground, Bath *above & left*

Close to the river Avon, the Recreation Ground has been hosting Somerset matches since 1880. The opening county match staged there was against Yorkshire in 1898. Somerset have an historic association with the ground, even though it is better known as the home of Bath Rugby Club. The ground is owned by the local authority, and, as well as the rugby ground, it also has a sports and leisure centre. Memorable performances include 303 not out from the Australian batsman Warwick Armstrong for the tourists in a match against Somerset in 1903. In more recent times, Mike Gatting dominated the home attack, scoring a career-best 258 for Middlesex in 1984.

Alec Stewart on The Oval:

"I have always loved everything about The Oval. People may say it is not the prettiest ground, but for me The Oval is right up there as a special venue – in particular the pitches and the overall quality of the square. My relationship with the ground began as a small child; in fact I first went there as a two-year-old when Dad played there for Surrey. My first first-class match at The Oval was against Oxford University in 1983. My very last match was at The Oval in September 2003 for England against South Africa. We won the match to square the series, and I was given a fabulous send-off by the Surrey members and England fans. Unfortunately I never managed a Test century there, but I did get a one-day hundred for England, and my highest first-class score of 271 not out. For me, The Oval is home from home and I was delighted and honoured when they named the gates after me at the Vauxhall End."

SURREY

It is apparent from a reference to "creckett" in a legal document dating from 1550 that cricket has been played in Surrey for almost 500 years. The Surrey club was formed in 1845, and has from the outset been based at The Oval. Under the captaincy of Frederick Miller, and boasting leading players such as William Caffyn and Julius Caesar, Surrey was recognised as Champion County seven times in the 1850s.

Thirty years later, the second of Surrey's golden ages occurred, inspired by the captaincy of John Shuter and his successor, KJ Key. In 1887, 1888 and (jointly) 1889 it was Champion County. In 1890 Surrey was the first winner of the modern Championship, a crown it was to hold a further five times in the 1890s. The batting was led by the high-scoring Bobby Abel – who made nine double centuries at The Oval, once carrying his bat through the innings for 357 not out, which remains the highest score by a Surrey player – and Tom Hayward, a stylish batsman, the first of five Surrey men to score 100 hundreds and whose 3,246 runs for Surrey in 1906 remain a county record. The key bowlers were George Lohmann, who in 18 Tests took 112 wickets at the phenomenally low average of 10.75, the tireless paceman Tom Richardson, who in the space of just four seasons took more than 1,000 wickets, and all-rounder Bill Lockwood, who 13 times took eight or more wickets in an innings for Surrey.

The successes of the 1890s were not experienced again for 50 years. Surprisingly, in his illustrious 30-year Surrey career the great Sir Jack Hobbs was only once a member of a Championship-winning side, in 1914, although several times his club came very close. Whilst the batting, starting with Hobbs and Andrew

COUNTY RECORDS

Formed in 1845
County Champions 1890, 1891, 1892, 1894, 1895, 1899, 1914, 1950 (shared), 1952, 1953, 1954, 1955, 1956, 1957, 1958, 1971, 1999, 2000, 2002
Gillette/NatWest/C&G/FP 1982
Benson & Hedges 1974, 1997, 2001
Sunday League 1996, 2003
Twenty20 2003
Nickname of one-day team Brown Caps

Leading run-scorer Sir Jack Hobbs (1905-34) 43,554 (av 49.72)
Leading wicket-taker Tom Richardson (1892-1904) 1,775 (av 17.87)
Most wicket-keeping dismissals Herbert Strudwick (1902-27) 1,221 (1,035 ct, 186 st)
Most capped England player Alec Stewart (1981-2003) – 133 Tests

COUNTY GROUND AVERAGES
Average first innings total in first-class matches 355
Average runs per wicket in first-class matches 36.05
Average runs per over in limited overs matches 5.53

Sandham, was very strong, and the respected Herbert Strudwick kept wicket, the bowling was weak. It required all of the ingenuity and boldness of Surrey's canny leg-spinning captain, Percy Fender, to bowl other sides out on the batsman-friendly Oval wickets. Nor did Fender's successor as captain, England's "Bodyline" skipper Douglas Jardine, manage to overcome Surrey's bowling deficiencies, despite the hard-working paceman Alf Gover, who took more than 200 wickets in both 1936 and 1937.

It was Surrey's formidable bowling attack which was the primary reason for their unequalled domination of the Championship in the 1950s. After sharing the spoils in 1950, from 1952 Surrey won seven Championships in a row, the first five under the leadership of Stuart Surridge, the last two under the team's leading bat, Peter May. The bowling was opened by the great Alec Bedser and by Peter Loader, who in 1958 took 9-17 at The Oval against Warwickshire; the spin bowling was in the hands of Jim Laker, whose feat of taking 19 Ashes wickets at Old Trafford in 1956 is unapproached in all first-class cricket, and the combative Tony Lock, with the capable support of Bedser's twin brother Eric. Wonderful support in the field was provided by wicket-keeper Arthur McIntyre and fearless fielders in the leg-trap, notably Lock and Micky Stewart. In 1956 Surrey won 23 of its 28 Championship matches – and was the first county for 44 years to defeat the Australians.

Between 1959 and 1999 Surrey won the Championship only once, in 1971 under Micky Stewart's captaincy. This was despite the emergence of John Edrich and Ken Barrington as bulwarks of England's batting, and of seamers Geoff Arnold and Robin Jackman – whose 121 wickets in 1980 helped the county to finish runners-up – and off-spinner Pat Pocock; and the fearsome pace of West Indian quicks Sylvester Clarke and Tony Gray.

At the turn of the millennium Surrey once

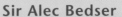

COLLECTOR-CRICKET - A.V. Bedser at The Oval.
Photograph: Surrey County Cricket Club

Sir Alec Bedser

Born in 1918, Sir Alec Bedser lays strong claim to being the greatest of all fast-medium bowlers. Indistinguishable from his identical twin brother Eric – who played for Surrey as an all-rounder between 1939 and 1962, scoring 14,716 runs and taking 833 wickets in his career – Sir Alec took 11 wickets in each of his first two Tests, and ended up with a then world-record 236 wickets in 51 Tests. His 39 wickets in the series helped England regain the Ashes in 1953. Bedser dismissed Sir Donald Bradman six times in Tests, including (uniquely) twice for a duck, and once with a fast leg-cutter which Bradman reckoned was the best ball he ever faced. Sir Alec retired with 1,924 wickets – 715 of them (av 18.67) at The Oval – after which he was an England selector for 23 years (chairman for 12 of them) and President of Surrey. The Bedser twins were vital elements of the Surrey team which won seven successive Championships in the 1950s. Both of them played in the game between Surrey and Old England in May 1946 to which Sir Alec refers below: the two men he dismissed – Patsy Hendren, then aged 57 (for 94) and Frank Woolley, aged 59 (for 62) – boasted a combined total of 116,000 runs and 315 centuries (and 116 years!)

Sir Alec Bedser on The Oval:

"I have many recollections of The Oval. It is now over 70 years since Eric and I first walked through the Jack Hobbs Gates to start our careers as young pros. That is one of my most vivid memories, as being a cricketer was always something we both wanted to do. The Oval was a great ground to be associated with – so much tradition. I particularly remember playing in the match for Surrey against Old England (pictured below) in May 1946, in front of a crowd of some 18,000, including King George VI. It was a great day – the first big match at The Oval after the War. We agreed not to appeal for lbws. It would have been foolish not to allow so many people not to see these old players score runs. When they got in you could see what great players they had been. Eric and I played a trick on the great Frank Woolley. He had not seen us before, so he did not know we were twins. I bowled the first three balls of one over to him at medium pace, and Eric completed the over with slow off-breaks. Woolley (thinking that all six balls had been bowled by the same person) expressed astonishment at the bowler's versatility!"

The Old England team: back row, Hobbs (Umpire), Holmes, Allom, Tate, Brooks, Sandham, Strudwick (Umpire); middle row, Hendren, Jardine, Fender, Sutcliffe, Woolley; front row, Knight, Freeman.

again dominated the county scene, under the inspirational captaincy of Adam Hollioake, aided by coach Keith Medlycott. As well as winning the Championship in 1999, 2000 and 2002, Surrey captured several one-day trophies, with key contributions from Martin Bicknell and Mark Ramprakash, neither of whom, despite remarkable achievements for Surrey year after year, found much favour with the England selectors. Surrey's aura of success was dented by demotion to the Championship's Division Two in 2005. Whilst promotion as Division Two champions followed the next year, in 2008 Surrey finished bottom of Division One and, for the first time in its proud history, failed to register a single Championship victory.

The Oval

When, in 1844, the Montpelier Cricket Club of Walworth needed a new ground its treasurer, William Baker, arranged for it to obtain a 31-year lease (for £140 per year) of the market garden at Kennington Oval, which was – and remains to this day – owned by the Duchy of Cornwall. Ten thousand pieces of turf, purchased from Tooting Common, were laid, and the first cricket

matches were played soon afterwards. The ground took its name not from its own shape but from that of the streets surrounding it. Since the early 1850s the nearby gasholders have provided a distinctive backdrop.

The development of the cricket ground helped inspire the formation of Surrey County Cricket Club in 1845. The Oval became its base. In 1880 Surrey secretary CW Alcock arranged for the first Test Match in England to be played at The Oval, when 40,000 spectators watched England, for whom WG Grace scored 152, defeat Australia by five wickets. Two years later, The Oval witnessed England's first defeat by Australia – a loss which proved the inspiration for the Ashes.

In its early days The Oval hosted important events for several other sports, including the first FA Cup Final in 1872 – further finals were held there between 1874 and 1892 – the first England soccer international and the first rugby fixtures England played against Wales and Scotland.

The renewal of the lease in 1896 prompted Surrey to build its present pavilion, designed by architect Thomas Muirhead, who had previously designed the Old Trafford pavilion. Over the years

The Oval became more dilapidated – during the Second World War it was converted for use as a prisoner-of-war camp but never used for this role. Recently, considerable redevelopment has taken place, including the destruction of the north stands at the Vauxhall End and their replacement by the OCS Stand, which was opened in 2005, and the installation of four 130ft-high permanent floodlights. Financial difficulties have been mitigated by commercial sponsorship deals which have caused the Kennington Oval to be renamed the Fosters Oval, then the AMP Oval and, now, the Brit Oval. Ambitious future plans include the demolition of the Surrey Tavern and the creation of a "piazza" between Harleyford Road and the pavilion. The pavilion will then be the centrepiece of the entrance to the stadium. A new combined stand and hotel will then be constructed to the north of the pavilion.

The Oval has a reputation as a batting paradise – more than 135 double centuries have been scored there, including Len Hutton's famous 364 in England's record total of 903 for 7 in the 1938 Ashes Test – but it has also seen famous bowling achievements – including Eric Hollies' bowling Bradman for a duck in his last Test innings in 1948, and Michael Holding's 14 wickets for West Indies in the 1976 Oval Test. Since The Oval traditionally hosts the last Test of the summer, the ground has seen some famous series-deciding matches, including those in 1926, 1953 and 2005 which resulted in England regaining the Ashes, each time after more than a decade of Australian domination.

THE OVAL

Address Surrey County Cricket Club
Kennington
London SE11 5SS
Main tel 08712 461100
Website www.surreycricket.com

Ends Pavilion End, Vauxhall End
Capacity 23,000
First County Match Surrey v Kent
(25 June 1846)
First Test Match England v
Australia (6 September 1880)
First ODI England v
West Indies
(7 September 1973)
Record crowd 80,000
(over the course of a 3-day match)
Surrey v Yorkshire (26 July 1906)

Scoreboard

Pavilion
(QS) Stand

OCS (South)
Stand

Vauxhall End

Pavilion End

Pavilion

Scoreboard

KENNINGTON OVAL

FAMOUS PLAYERS

Sir Jack Hobbs and Andrew Sandham

For 15 years after the First World War Sir Jack Hobbs (1882-1963) and Andrew Sandham (1890-1982) were Surrey's opening batsmen. They shared in 66 century first-wicket stands, the highest of which, 428 against Oxford University in 1926, remains a Surrey record. Hobbs was regarded by many as the finest batsman ever on all wickets. Although not himself statistically-minded, he scored more runs (61,237) and more centuries (197) than anyone else. He made 90 of his hundreds at The Oval – no man has scored as many at one ground – but only two in a Test Match at The Oval, one of them his famous innings of 100 on a sticky wicket in 1926 which helped England to win the Ashes. The first professional cricketer to be knighted, Hobbs was admired for his integrity and personal modesty. Hobbs' highly-successful opening partnership with Herbert Sutcliffe for England limited Sandham's opportunities at Test level to 14 matches over nine years, and he was never given the chance to open the batting with Hobbs in a Test Match. Nevertheless, Sandham signed off from Test cricket in style, scoring 325 and 50 in his last Test, against the West Indies at Kingston in 1929-30. For Surrey, Sandham was a faithful servant, amassing 10 double centuries for the county, and making the last of his 107 hundreds in his last match for the county in 1937. Surrey coach during the county's remarkable run of success in the 1950s, he then became county scorer, a post he only relinquished in 1970, at the age of 80.

Raman Subba Row

Born in 1932, Raman Subba Row enjoyed batting at The Oval, where he scored 1,664 runs at an average of 59.42. Only four men – Mark Ramprakash, Sir Len Hutton, Herbert Sutcliffe and Wally Hammond – have exceeded 1,500 runs at that ground with a higher average. A member of Surrey's Championship-winning teams of 1953 and 1954 Subba Row went on to captain Northamptonshire, for whom he scored 300, a then county record, against his old county at The Oval in 1958, sharing a partnership of 376 with Albert Lightfoot which remains to this day the ground's record sixth wicket stand. At the age of just 29 he retired from cricket to go into business:

in the last of his 13 Tests, the 1961 Oval Ashes Test, the left-hander scored 137. Subsequently Chairman of Surrey and Chairman of the TCCB, he was manager of the 1981-82 England tour to India.

Raman Subba Row on The Oval:

"The Oval has special memories for me, starting with the Young Amateurs matches in 1949, when I played there as a schoolboy incapable of believing that I was batting on the same ground that Jack Hobbs and Don Bradman had batted on. Super pitch, lovely arena and a magic atmosphere.

Little did I know then that I would be back after Cambridge University at the invitation of skipper Stuart Surridge in 1953 to join a Championship-winning side with Peter May, Jim Laker and Tony Lock. But the crowning glory came eight years later, when I scored a Test century against the Australians, who had Richie Benaud, Neil Harvey and Alan Davidson in their side, along with many other names who have remained life-long friends. After retirement as a player, I joined the Surrey committee in the 1960s and with Bernie Coleman started the marketing exercises which led to my being invited to be Club Chairman in the 1970s for five years and then Chairman of the TCCB in the 1980s for a similar period. I owe the lovely Oval so much!"

Micky & Alec Stewart

Father and son duo Micky (born 1932) and Alec Stewart (born 1963) were Surrey stalwarts between 1954 and 2003. Both scored a little over 26,000 runs in their careers, both fell just short of 50 first-class hundreds (Micky made 49, Alec 48), and both, fittingly, made their highest scores at The Oval: Alec, 271 not out against Yorkshire in 1997, Micky, 227 not out against Middlesex in 1964. Both also made important contributions in the field. Micky was a brilliant short-leg fielder who took 77 catches in 1957, including a world-record seven catches in one innings, and ended up with more catches for Surrey – 605 – than any other fielder. He played 8 Tests, averaging 35 with the bat; he had to withdraw at tea on the first day of what transpired to be his last Test, at Bombay in 1963-64, with dysentery, which necessitated his early return from the tour. Between 1963 and 1972 he captained Surrey. He went on to manage Surrey and England. Alec kept wicket for 82 of his England-record 133 Tests, in which he scored 8,463 runs and made 277 dismissals. He scored 118 and 143 in the Barbados Test of 1993-94 and a century in his 100th Test – appropriately, since he is a royalist, on the late Queen Mother's 100th birthday! In 1998 and 1999, he found himself captaining England, opening the batting and keeping wicket. A fluent stroke-maker, Alec scored 4,677 runs in 170 one-day internationals.

Micky Stewart on The Oval:

"The first time I saw The Oval was as a seven-year-old nipper in 1939. On the tram on the way to town, we

saw long grass and barbed wire: it had been converted to a prisoner-of-war camp. My playing career there was between 1954 and 1972, the last decade as captain. In my first match at The Oval, I scored a fifty against Gloucestershire and followed this with a hundred in my second match there, against the touring Pakistanis. Such was the strength of the Surrey bowling attack at the time that it was not until my third season that a visiting team scored more than 300. I played in five of the seven Championship-winning sides of the 1950s. Memorable moments were the times we won the Championship; four of the five titles when I was in the team were clinched in matches at The Oval."*

John Edrich

John Edrich (born 1937) was a compact left-handed opening batsman four of whose cousins, including the Middlesex and England all-rounder Bill Edrich, played county cricket. He captained Surrey between 1973 and 1977 and England for one Test, but is best known for his courageous batting, which between 1956 and 1978 yielded almost 40,000 runs and 103 hundreds. In 77 Tests his highest score was 310 not out against New Zealand in 1965 on a seaming Headingley wicket, an innings which included five sixes and 52 fours. A mark of his tenacity is his batting average against the most uncompromising of opponents, Australia: 48.96. Edrich made 39 hundreds at The Oval, the highest of them an

unbeaten 226 against Middlesex in 1967. Since 2006 he has been President of Surrey.

John Edrich on The Oval:

"I first went to The Oval in 1954 as a 17-year-old. When I walked in I was amazed by the sheer size of the ground. The square was very large – something I had never seen before, coming from a small club ground in Norfolk. In the old days we used the whole field. If a batsman hit the ball towards the Vauxhall Stand, such were the distances he could run 5. My first match at The Oval for Surrey was in the 1958 season against Worcestershire. Surrey had already won the Championship that season; the last year of a remarkable seven-year Championship-winning run. I was to play at The Oval for over 20 years. One of my particular highlights was the 164 I scored in the Ashes Test at The Oval in 1968. Because of its traditional place in the cricket calendar as the venue of the final Test of the summer, the Oval Test has often decided the outcome of a series. This has led to some wonderful matches, including memorable Ashes contests in 1953, 1968 and, of course, 2005."

OTHER GROUNDS

Guildford Cricket Club *above*

Cricket has been played on the Woodbridge Road Ground since the 1870s, and the ground was donated to the council by Sir Harry Waechter in 1911. A record crowd of 7,000 attended one of the days of Surrey's first game there, in 1938; save for a period in the 1960s, Surrey has played there ever since.

The only permanent structures are the two-storey pavilion and the scoreboard, which was modelled on that of the Sydney Cricket Ground. The seating is temporary. The ground is surrounded by trees. Its long, narrow shape and small size has encouraged fast scoring, notably Justin Langer's 342 for Somerset in 2006 and Ali Brown's 203 in a Sunday League game against Hampshire in 1997.

The Bicknell brothers enjoyed playing on their local ground: in 2000 Martin took 7-72 and 9-47 against Leicestershire, to record the second-best match figures in Surrey's history; whilst Darren's 228 not out against Nottinghamshire in 1995 was a ground record until eclipsed by Langer.

Whitgift School *not pictured*

The Whitgift School ground has hosted Surrey matches since 2000, when a Sunday League match was held there to celebrate the independent boys' school's 400th anniversary. Helped by the fact that a good proportion of Surrey's membership live in Croydon, Whitgift has been awarded Championship games since 2003. Mark Ramprakash has made three centuries on the ground – no-one else has scored more than one – including by some distance the highest score made there, 279 not out against Nottinghamshire in 2003.

Whitgift, whose cricket coach is the former Surrey batsman David Ward and whose alumni include Raman Subba Row, boasts excellent indoor nets and has become the base for Surrey's cricket academy. Its only permanent building is the pavilion, but spectators can sit on a huge grass bank which is covered by high trees.

COUNTY RECORDS

Formed in 1839
County Champions 2003, 2006, 2007
Gillette/NatWest/C&G/FP 1963, 1964, 1978, 1986, 2006
Benson & Hedges Best – Semi-finals 1982, 1999
Sunday League 1982, 2008
Twenty20 Best – Semi-finals 2007
Nickname of one-day team Sharks

Leading run-scorer John Langridge (1928-55) 34,150 (av 37.69)
Leading wicket-taker Maurice Tate (1912-37) 2,211 (av 17.41)
Most wicket-keeping dismissals Harry Butt (1890-1912) 1,176 (911 ct, 265 st)
Most capped England player Ted Dexter (1957-68) – 62 Tests

COUNTY GROUND AVERAGES
Average first innings total in first-class matches 343
Average runs per wicket in first-class matches 33.11
Average runs per over in limited overs matches 4.89

Jim Parks on the County Ground, Hove:
"Hove was a very happy hunting ground for me. I always enjoyed the atmosphere there – very relaxing – and in the old days when batting at the top end you had a lovely view of the sea. One of my happiest memories of the Hove ground was in 1963, the first year of the Gillette Cup, when in the quarter-final I managed to win the Man of the Match award by smashing Yorkshire for a quick 90. We did, of course, go on to win the Cup in its first year."

SUSSEX

Cricket has been played in Sussex for hundreds of years but it is only since the turn of the 21st century that the Hove-based county has won the County Championship, becoming one of the most successful teams of the decade.

It is apparent from ecclesiastical court records that cricket was played in Sussex as long ago as 1611 – two parishioners were fined and made to do penance for playing cricket instead of attending church on Easter Sunday – and the county club, founded in 1839, is England's oldest county cricket club. Prior to 1855 Sussex won the unofficial championship seven times and shared it once. However, the club had to wait until 2003 to win the official County Championship. After finally breaking its duck, it became the dominant county and won the Championship again in 2006 and 2007 – on the latter occasion only by 4.5 points on the last day of the season after Lancashire failed by just 25 to reach a mammoth 489 to beat Surrey.

Just as the main reason for Sussex's historic failure to win the Championship was their relative weakness in bowling, so it is striking that the most significant contributions to their Championship triumphs were made by the Pakistan leg-spinner Mushtaq Ahmed. The leading Championship wicket-taker for each of the years 2003 to 2007, he took 459 wickets in those five seasons. Most tellingly, he took 83 wickets in Sussex's 10 wins in 2003; 80 in the nine victories in 2006; and 60 in the seven games they won in 2007. Bowling support was provided by James Kirtley; the star batsman was the Zimbabwean Murray Goodwin, who in the Championship-sealing defeat of Leicestershire in 2003 made the highest-ever score for Sussex, 335 not out.

In the early 20th century, Sussex had an immensely powerful batting line-up, headed by Ranjitsinhji and CB Fry. In 1901 Sussex made six totals of more than 500 and the first-class

THE COUNTY GROUND, HOVE

Scoreboard

Cromwell Road End

Sea End

Members' Pavilion

Scoreboard

Address County Ground
Eaton Road, Hove BN3 3AN
Main tel 01273 827100
Website www.sussexcricket.co.uk

Ends Cromwell Road End, Sea End
Capacity 7,000 for Twenty20
(otherwise 4,000)

First County Match Sussex v
Gloucestershire (6 June 1872)
First ODI India v South Africa
(15 May 1999)
Record crowd 7,800 India
v South Africa (15 May 1999)

averages were headed by three Sussex men, all of whom averaged over 70 – Fry (who made 13 hundreds), George Brann and Ranjitsinhji. Ranjitsinhji led the county to second place in the Championship in 1902 and 1903, but the bowling, despite the spin of Fred Tate and George Cox senior, was not quite strong enough for Sussex to finish top.

In the 1920s Sussex were led by Arthur Gilligan. For a short time he and Maurice Tate formed the most devastating bowling attack in the country. Whilst Gilligan's effectiveness was blunted by a blow over the heart when batting, the tireless Tate went on to carry the bowling attacks of both Sussex, for which he took more wickets than any other bowler, and England, for whom he took 155 wickets in 39 Tests. A more than useful bat, Tate also scored more than 17,000 runs for Sussex alone.

Sussex enjoyed a golden period in the early 1930s, finishing second in the Championship in 1932, 1933 and 1934. Their nucleus consisted of members of cricketing families who have served Sussex remarkably well over the years: the batting of Duleepsinhji (Ranjitsinhji's nephew), John Langridge, Harry Parks and George Cox junior and the all-round contributions of James Langridge (John's brother) and Harry Parks' brother Jim, who in 1937 performed a unique double by scoring 3,003 runs and taking 101 wickets.

After a poor start following the Second World War, in 1953

David Sheppard led Sussex to second place again. Unfortunately neither he nor Hubert Doggart (who captained the side in 1954) was able to play for Sussex for more than one full season. Between 1960 and 1965 Sussex were captained by Ted Dexter, who led them to Gillette Cup triumphs in the first two years of that competition; Sussex were losing finalists in three of the next 10 years. As well as the powerful hitting of Dexter and wicket-keeper Jim Parks junior, important contributions were made by all-rounder Alan Oakman, paceman John Snow and medium-pacer Ian Thomson.

Under the astute captaincy of John Barclay, in 1981 Sussex, agonisingly, were pipped to second place in the Championship by just two points, but they went on to win the Sunday League the following year and the NatWest Trophy in 1986. However, despite the all-round skills of Imran Khan and the batting of Alan Wells, the county had to wait two further decades before Chris Adams led them to three Championships – and the C&G Cup in 2006 and the Sunday League title in 2008.

sea. The sea fret helped bowlers such as Maurice Tate and Imran Khan to swing the ball prodigiously. Spinners have also enjoyed themselves at Hove: Kent leg-spinner "Tich" Freeman had remarkable innings figures of 9-11 in 1922, and he ended up taking 17 wickets in the match for just 67 runs.

On the other hand, on a hot and cloudless day batsmen have caused carnage, including Duleepsinhji and Eddie Paynter, both of whom performed the rare feat of scoring more than 300 runs in a day, and Murray Goodwin, who scored a club record 335 not out in 2003. In 1984 Viv Richards hit a six over the Arthur Gilligan Stand – the ball carried for 130 yards. However, the most famous innings at Hove was played by Nottinghamshire's Edwin Alletson, who in 1911 despite an injured wrist scored a remarkable 189 in 90 minutes, during which he hit 34 runs off one over and 97 in just five overs. One of Alletson's eight sixes smashed the pavilion clock; another damaged the pavilion bar. He scored 142 of the 152 put on for the last wicket in just 40 minutes. Remarkably, it was the only hundred of his career.

The County Ground, Hove

The ground at Eaton Road has been the home of Sussex cricket for almost 140 years. When it was purchased in 1871 it was a barley field, but the turf was removed from the club's previous Royal Brunswick Ground and relaid at Eaton Road, where it has remained ever since.

There is a slope towards the Sea End, and the ground is surrounded on two sides by tall blocks of flats; the ball can be difficult to pick up against the background of the stands and flats. The large pavilion has grown piecemeal over the past 120 years or so, and contains many interesting photographs and items of cricketing ephemera.

Much of the seating on the northern end of the ground is deckchairs (in Sussex's blue and white colours), as befitting a ground which is a stone's throw from the

OTHER GROUNDS

Arundel Castle Ground *left*

Located near to Arundel Castle, this picturesque ground was built by the 15th Duke of Norfolk in 1895. In 1975 Lavinia, widow of the 16th Duke, decided to hold cricket matches as a tribute to her late husband. The custom arose of international touring teams playing their first match – a one-day friendly – at Arundel. In 1986 the Arundel Castle Cricket Foundation was established. Through the generosity of Sir Paul Getty, an indoor school was built behind the pavilion, which was opened by HRH Prince Charles in 1991 and both the indoor school and the ground have since been used by hundreds of young, and blind and partially-sighted, cricketers.

Cricket Field Ground, Horsham

Horsham Cricket Club was formed as long ago as 1771. Since 1854 it has played at the ground known for the appropriately named road on which it is located as the Cricket Field Road Ground. Sussex have played at the ground since 1908, although no County Championship matches took place there between 1957 and 1982. Horsham now hosts a festival week in June, featuring one four-day and one one-day match.

This picturesque village ground is overlooked by the spire of St Mary's church, the ringing of whose bells accompanies the play. Its only permanent structure is the pavilion, built in 1921. For the annual festival, temporary marquees are erected. Perhaps the most notable cricketing feat performed at Horsham was the bowling performance of George Cox senior on his home ground in 1926. Against Warwickshire he took 9-50 and 8-56: his match figures of 17-106 remain the best ever by a Sussex player. Not a bad performance for a bowler then aged 52!

Dennis Lillee

Born in Perth, Western Australia in 1949, Dennis Lillee was the spearhead of the Australian bowling attack for a decade. In his early days a tearaway fast bowler – in 1971-72 he destroyed a powerful World XI line-up with figures of 8 for 29 – he overcame several injuries to play 70 Tests, in which he took 355 wickets (av 23.92), a record 95 of them caught by wicket-keeper Rodney Marsh, who also finished up with 355 Test dismissals. In the 1981 Ashes series he took 39 wickets.

Dennis Lillee on Arundel:

"What makes Arundel so special is that it has always staged the pipe-opener for an Ashes tour. Arundel is just one of many picturesque grounds around England, but playing there and being part of something that only those selected for an Australian tour of England could experience certainly made you feel excited, yet apprehensive, about not only the game, but the commencement of another Ashes series.

I remember my first tour to England in 1972, and I can't tell you the anticipation of arriving at the ground, which had been steeped in history and part of Ashes folklore. It was freezing cold, and many of the Australian players were wearing thermals, flannels and singlets, while some wore up to three woollen jumpers plus tracksuit bottoms underneath their creams! This "big look" added to the aura of the Aussies taking on the Poms for what was, at the time, considered to be the greatest prize on offer in world cricket."

FAMOUS PLAYERS

CB Fry

CB Fry (1872-1956) was described by John Arlott as "probably the most variously gifted Englishman of any age". A classical scholar who beat Sir John Simon and FE Smith to the top scholarship of a remarkable year at Wadham College, Oxford, he was a versatile and polished writer, whose nine books were finely, if not all wisely, written:

in his autobiography, published in 1939, he stressed what a favourable impression Adolf Hitler made on him when they met. Fry stood for Parliament three times, and claimed to have been offered the throne of Albania at Geneva in 1920 when attending the League of Nations as an adviser to the Indian delegation. For almost 40 years he and his wife ran a training ship, *Mercury*. Fry played football for England and an FA Cup Final for Southampton, rugby for the Barbarians, and equalled the world long-jump record. But his main sport was cricket: one of the leading batsmen of his day, with a correct – if stiff – style he ended up with 30,886 runs at an average, exceptional for its time, of over 50, and 94 centuries – including six in successive innings. He and Ranjitsinhji formed a formidable batting duo for Sussex, which Fry captained between 1904 and 1908. Fry captained England in six of his 26 Tests.

Alan Oakman

Born in 1930, Alan Oakman gave Sussex yeoman all-round service for more than 20 years. He used his great height of 6ft 6in to his advantage: as a front-foot batsman he could drive with great power balls which would have been too short for others, and as a bat-pad fielder with a remarkable reach. In the second of his two Tests, the famous 1956 Old Trafford Ashes Test, he made a major contribution to Jim Laker's unapproached 19 wickets by taking five close catches off his bowling. Also a useful off-break bowler, Oakman ended up with almost 22,000 runs, 736 wickets and almost 600 catches. After retiring as a player, Oakman became an umpire and then the Warwickshire coach.

Alan Oakman on the County Ground:
"I first played at Hove in 1948. Hove is where I performed a hat-trick v Somerset in 1952, scored my first century – always a milestone in any cricketer's life – against Derbyshire in 1955 and the following year carried my bat through the Sussex first innings v Lancashire reaching 137 not out against a bowling attack which included Statham, Tattersall, Hilton, Smith and Greenhough. I remember Hove on a warm sunny day with the smell of mown grass. A good cricket pitch to play strokes on, but one that also encouraged bowlers, particularly when it was green. Fielding in the middle, surrounded by 'belt and braces' built houses and members, some sound asleep in deckchairs, the view from the north end at slip enabled me to glance over the Maurice Tate Gates to the sun glistening on a calm sea. Where better to be? The one blot on the landscape was the building of the huge block of flats at the south end of the ground."

Jim Parks junior

Jim Parks junior, born in 1931, was the most illustrious member of a famous cricketing family. His father, Jim senior, and uncle, Harry, both scored 20,000 runs for Sussex; his son, Bobby, was the Hampshire, and later Kent, wicket-keeper. In all first-class cricket no grandfather, father and son have come close to the 61,999 runs which the two Jims and Bobby Parks scored, or the 2,219 dismissals which the three of them took. Jim junior started as an attractive middle-order batsman and fine cover-point fielder, and made his Test debut as a batsman. He made his highest score, 205 not out, against Somerset at Hove in 1955. In an emergency in 1958 Parks for the first time donned the keeper's gloves: he did so well that the following year he made 93 dismissals as well as scoring 2,313 runs.

He went on to play 46 Tests, scoring almost 2,000 runs and making 114 dismissals. A warm personality, he did not thrive as Sussex captain in 1967 and 1968; however, his fast-scoring batting was key to the county's one-day success. In 1973, after 24 years with Sussex, he moved to Somerset for four seasons, bringing his total aggregate to 36,673 runs, with 51 hundreds, and 1,181 dismissals.

Ted Dexter

A tall and regal figure – hence his nickname "Lord Edward" – Ted Dexter was a destructive batsman who thrillingly attacked the fastest of bowlers. Born in Milan, Italy in 1935, he played for and captained Cambridge University and Sussex – leading the county to its early one-day successes. He skippered England in 30 of his 62 Tests, in which he scored 4,502 runs (av 47.89). A more than useful fast-medium bowler, he took 419 first-class wickets – 66 of them in Tests – and returned his best figures of 7-24 at Hove. He stopped playing cricket full-time when just 30, but, after enjoying considerable success as an amateur golfer, returned as Chairman of the England Selectors between 1989 and 1993.

Ted Dexter on the County Ground:
"I commuted from Pimlico on the Brighton Belle (11.30 start!!). Usually it was sunny with a light breeze from the south west. The pitch was fickle. Sometimes it would swing and seam. Sometimes not. The Australians visited for a one-day match (65 overs a side). There was a sea fret and they feared all sorts of demons. Lovely Sussex bowled them out cheaply - but the ball never moved off the straight!! All in the mind."

Alan Wells

Born in 1961, Alan Wells was an elegant batsman who was unlucky to be picked only for one Test Match and a single one-day international – unlucky, too, having waited until he was almost 34 finally to be capped at Test level, to be dismissed by Curtly Ambrose first ball. Wells scored over 21,000 in his career, the highest of his 46 hundreds being 253 not out against Yorkshire in 1991. He captained Surrey between 1992 and 1996, after which he ended his career with Kent. The Wellses are one of the many Sussex cricketing families: Alan's brother Colin was an all-rounder who played two one-day internationals.

James Kirtley

Fast bowler James Kirtley (born 1975) made an immediate mark on Test cricket in 2003 when he destroyed the South African batting with figures of 6-34. He has since only played three more Tests, as well as 11 one-day internationals. A recall for the Twenty20 World Cup in 2007 was not a success: the Australians hit his one over for 17 runs. Kirtley was Man of the Match in the final of the 2006 C&G Cup, taking 5-27.

James Kirtley on the County Ground:
"The fact that the crowd are right up next to the boundary gives Hove a great atmosphere and makes you feel that much closer to the supporters. The deckchairs give the ground its identity and are very much in keeping with the seaside feel of the club and town. It gives a great identity to the south coast. When the sea mist rolls in, the ball does a bit, which is helpful for a seam bowler. It can be difficult for the young bowlers trying to cope with the slant from north to south. Bowling up the hill is a struggle, but there are rewards when the captain gives you the nod to come down."

WARWICKSHIRE

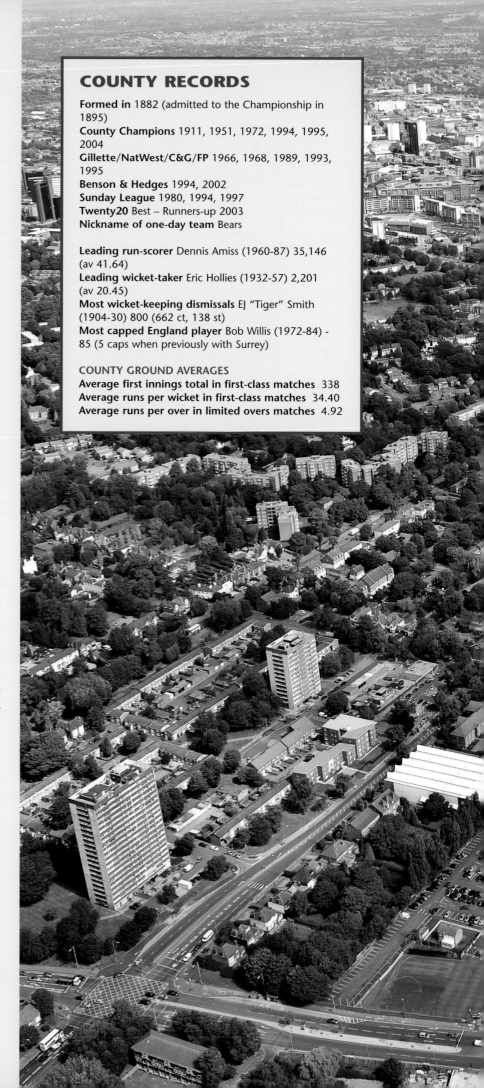

Warwickshire CCC was founded in 1882, an initiative led by schoolmaster William Ansell who helped the club to gain first-class status in 1894 and to join the Championship a year later. Since he also helped to establish Edgbaston as the county's ground, it is fitting that its west wing is called the William Ansell Stand.

Warwickshire's early results as a county were moderate, and in 1910 they finished third from bottom in the County Championship. It was therefore a great surprise that the following year in an unusually dry summer the county just pipped Kent to the Championship crown. Frank Foster not only proved an inspiring leader in his first year as captain, but contributed mightily with both bat (1,383 runs) and ball (116 wickets with his fast left-arm bowling). Other notable batting contributions were made by Willie Quaife, halfway through a long and illustrious county career, Septimus Kinneir and Crowther Charlesworth, all of whom passed 1,000 runs. Chief bowling support was provided by paceman Frank Field with 122 Championship wickets.

Problematically, Warwickshire's Championship crowns have not created ongoing momentum. The county slipped to mid-table in the three years leading up to the First World War, despite the fine efforts of Foster, who in 1914 made what remained, until Lara's 501 not out in 1995, the highest score for the county: 305 not out in just 260 minutes against Worcestershire. Tragically, in the First World War Foster's career ended, at the age of 26, when he was crippled in a car accident. During the 1920s Warwickshire did not enjoy any great success, the bowling being over-dependent on Harry Howell and the captain, the Hon. Frederick Gough-Calthorpe. Bob Wyatt led the county to fourth place in 1934, with strong bowling contributions from JH Mayer and

George Paine, but more fallow years followed – even though in 1946 leg-spinner Eric Hollies took a club-record 180 wickets – until in 1951 Warwickshire's first professional captain, Tom Dollery, led what he described as "an extraordinary team of ordinary cricketers playing purposeful cricket" to the county's

Bob Barber on Edgbaston:

"Edgbaston was special for me not because the Glamorgan tail kindly gave me my only first-class hat-trick nor for a happy pre-lunch session against the Aussies: Edgbaston was friendly; all the staff spoke to you, wished you luck and meant it; you walked on the field with high spirits and knew fun would be part of the day. And even 'black days' didn't stop committee man Cyril Goodway giving us a drink and letting us know that they knew tomorrow would be better. How easy to play in such an atmosphere."

EDGBASTON, BIRMINGHAM

Address County Ground, Edgbaston Road, Birmingham B5 7QU
Main tel 0870 062 1902
Website www.edgbaston.com

Ends Pavilion End, City End
Capacity 21,000
First County Match Warwickshire v Kent
(14 May 1894)
First Test Match England v Australia (29 May 1902)
First ODI England v Australia (28 August 1972)
Record crowd 32,000
England v West Indies
(30 May 1957)

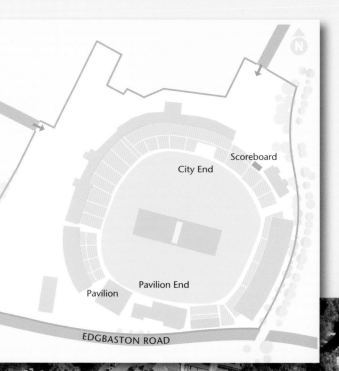

second Championship. Dollery, with almost 1,500 runs, led the batting, together with wicket-keeper Dick Spooner (who scored 1,767 runs and averaged 43); the chief bowling came from Hollies (145 wickets), Charlie Grove, who took 103 wickets in his farewell season, and New Zealand paceman Tom Pritchard (93 wickets).

Again, however, Warwickshire dropped off after a year of triumph. Under MJK Smith's captaincy between 1957 and 1967 there was an improvement. The captain's own brilliant batting in 1959, when he scored a club-record 2,417 runs, enabled the county to finish fourth. In 1964 it suffered the disappointment of being runners-up in both the Championship and the newly-instituted Gillette Cup. The carefree batting of Bob Barber and big-hitting Jim Stewart (who in a game against Lancashire at Blackpool in 1959 hit a then-record 17 sixes) was complemented by the disciplined pace bowling of Tom Cartwright, Jack Bannister and David Brown. The Gillette Cup was won in 1966.

Under the former England wicket-keeper Alan Smith, who over time recruited four formidable West Indians – stroke-makers Rohan Kanhai and Alvin Kallicharan, wicket-keeper Deryck Murray and off-spinner Lance Gibbs – Warwickshire won the Gillette Cup again in 1968, almost clinched the Championship in 1971, when Gibbs took a remarkable 131 wickets, and finally did so in 1972. Key contributors that season were the four West

Indian stars, Dennis Amiss (who averaged 66 with the bat), MJK Smith and fast bowler Norman McVicker – although the bowling averages were headed by Alan Smith, who had handed over the wicket-keeping gloves to Murray and took 20 wickets (average 22.45).

No further triumphs followed in the remainder of the 1970s. The highlight of Bob Willis' five years as captain between 1980 and 1984 was the Sunday League title in his first year as skipper. A steady decline followed, until under the guidance of coach Bob Woolmer and captain Dermot Reeve Warwickshire became, in the mid-1990s, the leading county in English cricket. After winning the NatWest Trophy in 1993, the following season Warwickshire enjoyed an *annus mirabilis*: it became the first county to win three of the four domestic trophies in a single season – and was the losing finalist in the fourth, the NatWest Trophy. While this was very much a team effort, the remarkable contribution of Brian Lara cannot be ignored: he scored 2,066 runs, averaged almost 90, and made the highest score in all first-class cricket, plundering the Durham attack to the tune of 501 not out.

Warwickshire retained the Championship in 1995, and won the C&G Trophy (the successor to the NatWest Trophy). Demotion from Division One of the Championship was swiftly followed by promotion back to the top flight – and a sixth Championship in 2004 under the leadership of Nick Knight, who won the toss in 13 of the county's 16 matches and scored a triple century against Middlesex. In a strong batting line-up which yielded 19 hundreds and 49 half-centuries, Ian Bell stood out with six centuries. Predictably, Warwickshire suffered demotion from both the Championship and Sunday League in 2007, but it bounced back as Division Two champions in 2008, helped by the inspired batting of reserve wicket-keeper Tony Frost, who came out of retirement to pass 1,000 runs and top the national averages with a batting average of 83.58.

Edgbaston, Birmingham

In 1884 Warwickshire took a 21-year lease of "a meadow of rough grazing land of around 12 acres at a fair and reasonable rental, without harrowing conditions" by the banks of the river Rea in the suburbs of Birmingham. They rented it from Lord Calthorpe, whose son, Frederick, captained the county throughout the 1920s. Further pieces of land were acquired over time, so that the ground is one of the largest in the UK: the site now covers 20 acres.

Edgbaston hosted its first Test Match in 1902. Although rain prevented a result, England dismissed Australia for just 36, Wilfred Rhodes taking 7-17. Just three Tests followed, in 1909, 1924 and 1929, until Test cricket returned to Edgbaston for good in 1957. The Edgbaston Test of 1957 was famous for the match-saving partnership of 411 between Peter May and Colin Cowdrey, who used their pads to nullify the threat of West Indies spinner Sonny Ramadhin. In 1974 came an even larger stand, when John Jameson (240 not out) and Rohan Kanhai (213 not out) put on an unbroken 465, the then world second-wicket record, against Gloucestershire. Twenty-one years later Brian Lara shaded all of the other notable batting feats performed at Edgbaston with his famous 501 not out, contributing the lion's share of a county record total of 810 for 4.

The return of Test cricket in 1957 followed extensive ground improvements, including the installation of the striking Thwaite Memorial Scoreboard. Erected in 1950 and subsequently transplanted to the City End it is named after Dr Harold Thwaite, a generous President of the Club. Energetic club fundraising helped to pay for the "Brumbrella", a huge motorised cover which protects the whole ground from rain.

Right: Brian Lara stands in front of the Edgbaston scoreboard after his record innings of 501 not out against Durham, 6 June 1994.

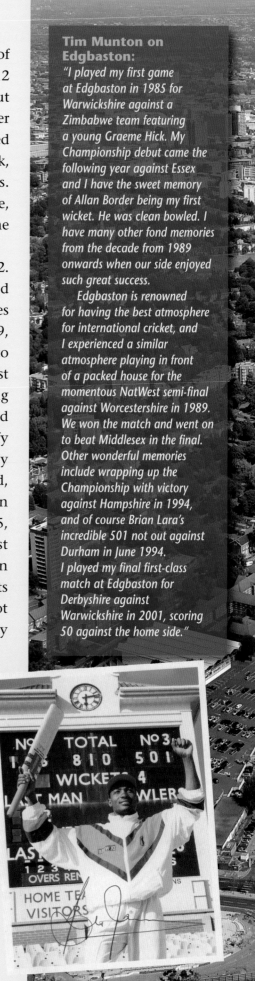

Dennis Amiss

Dennis Amiss (born 1943) first played for Warwickshire at the age of 17 in 1960. He retired 27 years later with more runs and centuries than any other Warwickshire player. A punishing batsman particularly noted for his cover-drive and leg-glance, in all first-class cricket he exceeded 43,000 runs, including 102 hundreds. In his 50-Test international career, Amiss endured some lows, especially against Australia, but was England's leading batsman between 1972 and 1974, in which period he scored over 2,000 runs and averaged 71. Once set, Amiss was difficult to dislodge: in eight of his 11 Test hundreds he went on to pass 150. A considerable one-day batsman, Amiss scored the first century in one-day international cricket, and averaged almost 48 in his 18 one-day internationals. Between 1994 and 2005 he was Warwickshire's chief executive. He is now vice-chairman of the English Cricket Board.

Dennis Amiss on Edgbaston:

"Edgbaston was my home ground. When it stages important matches there are big crowds and a wonderful atmosphere, and that was certainly the case during my playing days. The groundsman in my time was Bernard Flack, who prepared very good pitches – excellent batting pitches, which was ideal for batsmen like me but not so good for bowlers. Indeed it was a wonderful era for batsmen.

There were so many excellent batsmen there but no real openers so much to everyone's surprise I asked to open the batting. I had never opened before but Warwickshire had Alvin Kallicharan, Rohan Kanhai and MJK Smith. The first time I opened was at Edgbaston against Middlesex on an uncovered pitch. It was very wet yet I scored a big hundred against England bowlers John Price and Fred Titmus. It was not an easy pitch so I was pleased, and this innings was the launch-pad for my career as an opening bat for both Warwickshire and England.

I played several Tests at Edgbaston for England. My best innings was 86 not out against the West Indies in 1973. I think I would have gone on to make a century but stumps were drawn early because the match was clearly going to be a draw."

FAMOUS PLAYERS

Willie Quaife

A careful middle-order batsman and leg-spinner, Willie Quaife (1872-1951) served Warwickshire loyally for 35 years. With a height of 5ft 2in, he is thought to be the smallest cricketer to have played for England. He made his debut for Warwickshire in 1894, and signed off, at the age of 56, with 115 in his only innings of the 1928 season. In the meantime he scored more runs (33,862) and centuries (71) for Warwickshire than anyone else until Dennis Amiss broke both records shortly before his own retirement. Quaife was an excellent cover-point fielder, and a leg-break bowler who overcame concerns at the legality of his action to take 931 first-class wickets. Unfortunately, Quaife did not show his best form in international cricket, scoring just one fifty in his seven Tests. Early in his career Willie played a number of matches for Warwickshire with his older brother Walter; two decades later, he found himself sharing a dressing-room with his son Bernard. Remarkably, in the game between Warwickshire and Derbyshire at Derby in 1922, for a few overs the Quaifes faced the bowling of Billy Bestwick and his son Robert Bestwick.

MJK Smith

The last surviving English double-international, MJK Smith (born 1933) played rugby for England as a fly-half and 50 Tests as a forcing middle-order batsman especially strong on the leg-side. In half of those Tests he led the side with unflappable charm and marked selflessness. Smith was an equally popular captain of Warwickshire for a decade, leading the county to the Gillette Cup in 1966. Before joining Warwickshire in 1956 he had played a few games for Leicestershire and captained Oxford University, for whom he made centuries in all of his three Varsity Matches, including 201 not out in 1954. In the 1959 season Smith scored 3,249 runs, 1,209 of them in July alone. When he retired in 1975 he ended just short of 40,000 first-class runs. A brave short-leg fielder, he held a county record 52 catches in 1961. Smith was chairman of Warwickshire between 1991 and 2003, during which time his son Neil played for the county and in seven one-day internationals for England. When, in 1997, Neil captained the team it was the first time that a father and son had captained Warwickshire.

Lance Gibbs

Off-spin bowler Lance Gibbs (born 1934) was already an established Test star when he first played for Warwickshire in 1967, for whom he appeared until 1973. In 1971, his great season, he took 131 wickets (av 18.89). Only Malcolm Marshall in 1982 has exceeded that haul of wickets since the reduction in the county fixture list in 1969. In the following year Gibbs was an important member of the Championship-winning team. He enjoyed a long and illustrious Test career, taking a hat-trick against Australia and bowling out India at Barbados in 1961-62 with a remarkable spell of eight wickets in 15 overs for just six runs. In the last of his 79 Tests – his final first-class match – he overtook Fred Trueman's then-record haul of 307 Test wickets. Unlike his cousin Clive Lloyd, Gibbs was a poor batsman, and never reached 50 in first-class cricket.

Lance Gibbs on Edgbaston:

"Edgbaston is not as picturesque as Sabina Park in Jamaica or the Queen's Park Oval in Trinidad, but it's a ground where results are achieved. I had the privilege of playing at Edgbaston both for Warwickshire and for the West Indies against England. On the right side of the ground, near the main scoreboard, it is like playing and living in the Caribbean – thousands of West Indians enjoying their cricket and calypso as if they were at home.

I can recall some fantastic matches at that ground. Who will ever forget Sonny Ramadhin's magnificent spell in 1957 of 7-49, bowling out England for 186 – or the May-Cowdrey stand of 411 runs in England's second innings, in which Ramadhin bowled a world-record 98 overs? I also remember the third Test between England and the West Indies in 1963, when England won by 217 runs, Fred Trueman taking 7-44 in the West Indies' second innings, and Roy Fredericks' innings of 150 in the second Test of the 1973 series, with both sides playing not to lose.

When I joined Warwickshire in 1967 I remember Dennis Amiss telling me that I would not get 100 wickets in a season. I accomplished this in 1971 as early as the first week in August, and finished up with 131 wickets that season."

Bob Barber

Until 1963 Bob Barber (born 1935) was a cautious left-handed opening batsman for Lancashire, who did not enjoy being a young captain of the side, despite leading it to second place in the Championship in 1961. However, on his move to Warwickshire he blossomed into a thrilling stroke-maker, benefiting from the supportive captaincy of MJK Smith at both county and Test level. When Smith led the England tour of Australia in

1965-66, Barber scored more than 1,000 runs at a great pace, including a remarkable 185 in 255 balls on the first day of the Sydney Test, which remains the highest score by an Englishman on the first day of an Ashes Test. Barber was also a very useful, if under-used, leg-break bowler, who took more than 500 first-class wickets, including 42 in his 28 Tests. He retired from cricket in his early 30s to devote his energies to a successful business career.

Tim Munton

At 6ft 6in Tim Munton (born 1965) was a fast-medium bowler who played an important role in Warwickshire's triumphs in the mid-1990s. In 1994, as well as taking 81 wickets, Munton led the side, in the absence of the injured Dermot Reeve, for nine Championship games, of which eight were won. Munton played two Tests in 1992, and was voted Warwickshire's player of the season in 1990, 1991 and 1994, but suffered injury problems and played his last two seasons for Derbyshire before retiring in 2001. He ended up with 737 first-class wickets (av 25.86).

Ashley Giles

Originally a fast bowler, by the time Ashley Giles (born 1973) made his Warwickshire debut in 1993 he had, as a result of injury, become a slow left-arm bowler. A tall man, he extracted more bounce from the pitch than spin – Henry Blofeld famously described him as "wheely bin" because of his trundling run-up – and was a useful mid-to-late-order batsman. Although

his figures in his 54 Tests for England are not particularly impressive – his 1,421 runs came at an average of 20, half the cost of his 143 wickets – Giles made important contributions, including during the memorable 2005 Ashes series. Forced by injury to end his playing career in 2007, Giles is now Warwickshire's director of cricket.

Further developments followed, including the indoor Edgbaston Cricket Centre, an electronic scoreboard and the imposing Eric Hollies Stand, named after Warwickshire's leading wicket-taker. On Edgbaston's perimeter wall is the Sydney Barnes Wicket Gate: erected in 1973, on the centenary of his birth, it marks the place where the great bowler entered the ground in 1894 to play his first county match – and where his ashes were placed after his death in 1967. In the pavilion is located the Warwickshire County Cricket Club Museum, where many artefacts of county history are to be found. A major new £30m redevelopment of Edgbaston has been announced, intended to ensure that the ground meets ECB and ICC standards. The proposed redevelopment of one-third of the existing stadium will involve the construction of a new stand, thereby increasing the ground's capacity, currently 21,000, by another 5,000. It will also provide conference facilities, and will allow for the installation of permanent floodlights.

Tom Graveney

Tom Graveney (born 1927) joined Worcestershire in 1961 after his removal as Gloucestershire captain, and can be said to have turned a very good county side into a Championship-winning one. After finishing second in 1962, Worcestershire won the Championship in 1964 (when Graveney contributed 2,375 runs, av 55.23) and 1965. Graveney captained Worcestershire between 1968 and 1970, and scored 13,160 runs (av 46.01) for the county. In 1966 at the age of 39 he enjoyed a triumphant Test recall, playing important innings of 96, 109 and 165 against the West Indies. He went on to play 24 Tests between 1966 and 1969, ending up with 4,882 runs in 79 Tests (av 44.38) and 11 hundreds. In 2005 he became the first former professional cricketer to become MCC President.

Tom Graveney on New Road:

"The Worcestershire County Ground on New Road is one of the best grounds in the country – for me it is the best place I have ever played. It has a warm and welcoming feeling about it and the people that attend are very fair. One of the remarkable cricketing facts about the ground is that three Worcestershire players – Glenn Turner, Graeme Hick and I – have scored their 100th hundred there. Not a bad record!

On a day/night match one of the most beautiful sights is the floodlit cathedral in the background. Allied to all this is the care that the staff show to the people and players who come to this loveliest of grounds."

WORCESTERSHIRE

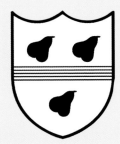

Founded in 1865, Worcestershire County Cricket Club joined the County Championship in 1899, after being Minor Counties Champions for each of the first four years of that competition. In the early days the county was so dominated by the Foster family that it became known as "Fostershire". Between 1899 and 1934 seven Foster brothers played for Worcestershire, and three captained the team. In 1899 RE Foster – whose 287 against Australia in 1903-04 remains the highest score by a Test debutant – and WL Foster each made two centuries in the same match for Worcestershire against Hampshire.

In 1907 Worcestershire finished in second place in the Championship. Thereafter, however, the club struggled. In geography and population the smallest of the first-class counties, it was nearly wound up in 1914, was unable to compete in the Championship in 1919 and in 1920 lost three successive county matches by an innings and more than 200 runs. Things only improved slightly in the next two decades despite the batting of Cyril Walters, "Doc" Gibbons and the Nawab of Pataudi senior. The team was also helped by the effective leg-theory bowling of Fred Root. Root took 207 wickets in 1925 and in 1931 (aged 41) returned figures of 9-23 against Lancashire, both of which remain Worcestershire records to the present day.

In the late 1940s Worcestershire developed a formidable bowling attack, with the fast-medium swing of Reg Perks – who took more wickets for Worcestershire than anyone else – and England spinners Dick Howorth and "Roly" Jenkins, which

COUNTY RECORDS

Formed in 1865 (admitted to the County Championship in 1899)
County Champions 1964, 1965, 1974, 1988, 1989
Gillette/NatWest/C&G/FP 1994
Benson & Hedges 1991
Sunday League 1971, 1987, 1988, 2007
Twenty20 Best – Quarter-finals 2004, 2007
Nickname of one-day team Royals

Leading run-scorer Don Kenyon (1946-67) 34,490 (av 34.18)
Leading wicket-taker Reg Perks (1930-55) 2,143 (av 23.73)
Most wicket-keeping dismissals Steve Rhodes (1985-2004) 1,095 (991 ct, 104 st)
Most capped England player Graeme Hick (1984-2008) – 65 Tests

COUNTY GROUND AVERAGES
Average first innings total in first-class matches 317
Average runs per wicket in first-class matches 31.34
Average runs per over in limited overs matches 4.73

enabled them to finish third in the Championship in 1949, a year in which Jenkins took 183 wickets.

Under the captaincy of Don Kenyon, Worcestershire won the Championship in 1964 and 1965, its centenary. Its batting had been strengthened by the recruitment of Tom Graveney and all-rounder Basil D'Oliveira, while the county's bowling attack – pacemen Flavell and Coldwell and spinners Gifford, Horton and Slade – provided many victims for wicket-keeper Roy Booth.

Heartened by one-day success, Worcestershire won the Championship again in 1974, with the help of the prolific batting of Glenn Turner and the astute captaincy of Norman Gifford. New recruits Ian Botham and Graeme Hick, who was to go on to score a record 106 hundreds for the county, inspired Worcestershire, led by Phil Neale, to two further Championship titles in the late 1980s and considerable one-day success.

Under the captaincy of Vikram Solanki, Worcestershire have again enjoyed one-day success. In 2007 they won the Sunday League, their first trophy for 13 years – but have experienced ups and downs in the Championship: in the last three years they have been promoted to Division One, demoted, and, finally in 2008 – Hick's last season – restored again to the top flight.

New Road

Worcestershire have played more than a thousand first-class matches at New Road, their home since 1899. Many consider New Road the most beautiful of all English grounds. It is instantly recognisable by virtue of its being overlooked by the 14th-century tower of Worcester Cathedral, which owned the ground until selling it to the club in 1976.

Three Worcestershire batsmen – Graveney, Turner and Hick – have exceeded 100 hundreds. Fittingly, all three made their 100th hundred at New Road, Turner going on to make a career-best 311 not out. Other batsmen who have enjoyed batting at New Road include the Middlesex opener Jack Robertson, who in 1949 made 331 not out in one day, and Don Bradman. In four innings in four games at Worcester – the curtain-raiser to each of his four tours of England – the Don massacred the Worcester bowling to the tune of 236 (1930), 206 (1934), 258 (1938) and 107 (1948).

Bowlers have also enjoyed success at New Road. Two – Glamorgan's Jack Mercer and Somerset's Jack White – have taken all 10 wickets in an innings there. Between 1983 and 1999 New Road hosted three one-day internationals. It has not held any internationals in recent years, despite its picturesque setting, at least in part because of its relatively limited crowd capacity.

In each of the 2007 and 2008 seasons New Road's proximity to the rivers Teme and Severn has caused it to suffer severe flooding. As a result, New Road has suffered serious damage, and games have been transferred to Kidderminster. Resisting calls for the club to move permanently from New Road, Worcestershire's chief executive, Mark Newton, pointed out, prosaically, that they couldn't move as "the ground is not worth anything".

Indeed, Worcestershire have underlined their commitment to New Road by embarking on a major redevelopment. The Members' Pavilion, which has been virtually unchanged since 1899, is to be replaced by the new

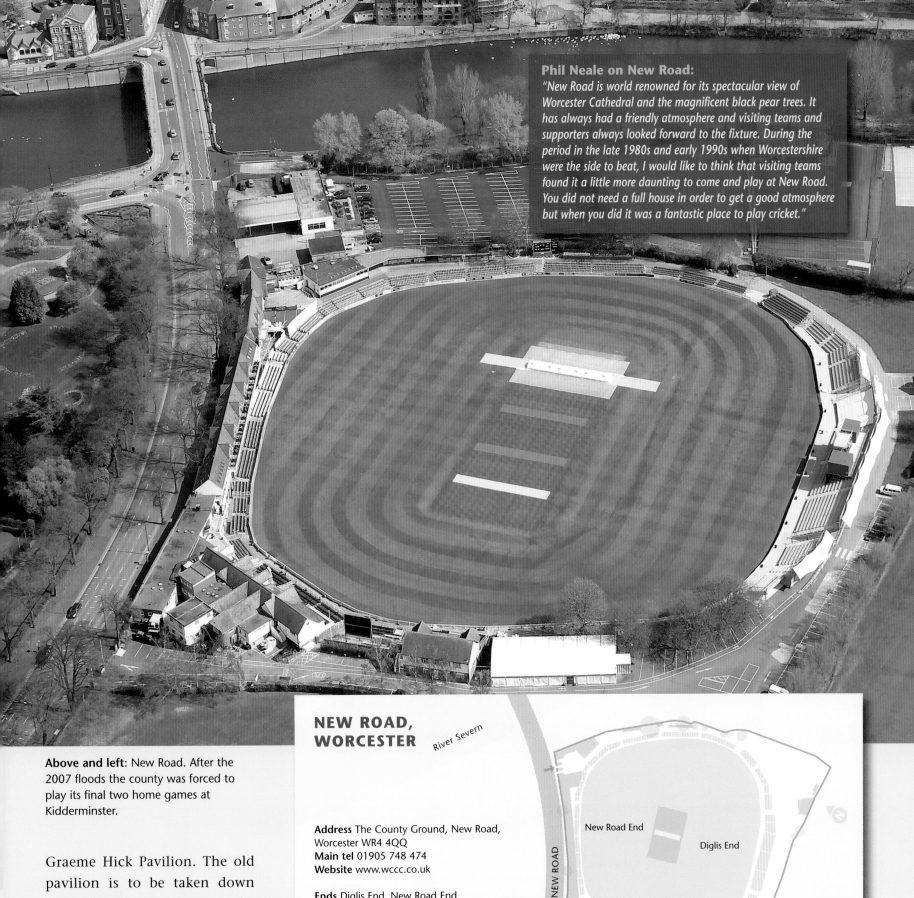

Above and left: New Road. After the 2007 floods the county was forced to play its final two home games at Kidderminster.

Graeme Hick Pavilion. The old pavilion is to be taken down brick-by-brick and rebuilt on the site of the Ladies' Pavilion, which is to be demolished. The new pavilion is to be built above the 1 in 150 year flood level, and will feature the Tom Graveney Lounge.

NEW ROAD, WORCESTER

Address The County Ground, New Road, Worcester WR4 4QQ
Main tel 01905 748 474
Website www.wccc.co.uk

Ends Diglis End, New Road End
Capacity 4,900
First County Match Worcestershire v Yorkshire (4 May 1899)
First ODI West Indies v Zimbabwe (13 June 1983)
Record crowd 32,000, (over 3 days) Worcestershire v the Australians (28–30 April 1948)

OTHER GROUNDS

Chester Road, Kidderminster

Cricket has been played at Chester Road since 1870. The home of Kidderminster Cricket Club (now called Kidderminster Victoria Cricket Club) since 1890, it hosted one county match a year between 1921 and 2002, except between 1974 and 1986.

Currently used for Worcestershire's Second XI matches, Chester Road has in the last two seasons stepped in, sometimes at very short notice, to hold several first team games when New Road has been unplayable owing to summer flooding. Indeed, in February 2008 Worcestershire signed a deal allowing county cricket to be transferred to Chester Road at 48 hours' notice in the event of flooding, in return for which the county agreed to invest £50,000 to improve the Chester Road ground's facilities.

Chester Road's old pavilion, which dated from 1870 and had been used for storing cricket equipment, was destroyed by a fire, believed to be caused by arson, in April 2008.

Worcestershire's most prolific batsman, Don Kenyon, made 259, the highest first-class score at Chester Road, in the match against Yorkshire in 1956 which attracted the ground's biggest crowd – 7,000. Eight years later, during the Championship-winning season of 1964, Jack Flavell took 9-56 against Middlesex, Chester Road's best bowling figures.

FAMOUS PLAYERS

RE Foster

Reginald Erskine Foster (1878-1914) was the greatest of the seven brothers who played for Worcestershire. A talented all-round sportsman he played eight Test Matches and five football internationals (scoring three goals) for England, and is the only man to have captained England at both sports. His sporting career was limited by pressures of business and the onset of diabetes, which led to his early death aged just 36. A batsman noted for his elegant off-driving and cutting, Foster is best known for the 287 he scored on his Test debut against Australia at Sydney in December 1903, which remained the highest Test score for more than 25 years. Although rarely able to play regularly for Worcestershire, when he could play he strengthened their batting considerably: in 1905 he did not bat for the county until August, but scored 246 in his first innings of the season.

Roy Booth

Wicket-keeper Roy Booth, born in 1926, was a key member of Worcestershire's Championship-winning sides of 1964 and 1965. He joined Worcestershire in 1956, after five years playing for his native Yorkshire, and became an ever-present member of the team into his 40s. Only seven wicket-keepers have ever made 100 dismissals in a season. Roy Booth is the last person to have performed that feat, and he did so twice, in 1960 and 1964. He ended up with 1,126 dismissals. His correct batting style was good enough to enable him to pass 1,000 runs in 1959 and to complete 10,000 career runs.

Roy Booth on New Road:
"My first game at Worcester was in 1953, when I was playing for Yorkshire, and I shared a partnership of 157 with Frank Lowson (who used to open the batting with Len Hutton). Frank scored 259 not out and I managed 53 not out – of course, at that time never thinking that I would be joining such a nice county in 1956. My first game for Worcester was perhaps less happy but a great occasion, the first game of the season against the Australians and the likes of Lindwall, Miller, Ian Johnson etc. I was lbw b Lindwall 0! Not a bad bowler to get a duck from! My last official innings was at Lord's in 1968 – ct Parfitt b Latchman 0. Not as illustrious a duck!"

Kapil Dev

In 2002 Kapil Dev (born 1959) was voted Wisden's Indian Cricketer of the Century, a fitting honour for India's finest all-rounder and best fast bowler. He led India to victory in the 1983 World Cup, playing an outstanding captain's innings which enabled India to win a crucial match against Zimbabwe: coming in at 17 for 5, he made 175 not out off 138 balls. In the 1990 Lord's Test he famously hit the last four balls of an over from Eddie Hemmings for six, enabling India to avoid the follow-on. In his 131 Tests between 1978 and 1994 he scored 5,248 runs (av 31.05) and took a then world-record 434 wickets (av 29.78), with best figures of 9-83 against the West Indies in 1983-84. Kapil Dev played for Haryana and county cricket for Northants (1981-83) and Worcestershire (1984-85). In 14 first-class matches at New Road he scored 877 runs (av 51.58) and took 44 wickets (av 25.77).

Kapil Dev on New Road:
"I thought that New Road was an ideal place at which to play cricket. It was a traditional cricket ground of the sort you would read about in the books. There were no large buildings, just a small pavilion – and a ladies' pavilion, where the games were watched by old ladies who used to bring cake and pastries to share with the cricketers. That's one of the things I used to love. New Road had beautiful surroundings, including the cathedral on one side. I enjoyed my two seasons there. I was a hard-hitting batsman and sometimes used to get some quick runs at New Road. I used to get to the ground at 9am and get a bit of sun on my body before the game started. The management were very nice – they took pride in the ground, and so did I."

Phil Neale

Phil Neale (born 1954) was an influential and highly successful captain of Worcestershire between 1982 and 1991, leading the club to two Championship titles, two Sunday League trophies and, in his last year as captain, the Benson & Hedges Cup. Also a professional footballer – his autobiography is called *A Double Life* – Neale played for Scunthorpe United alongside Ian Botham, whom he persuaded to move to New Road. A middle-order batsman, in his 18-year first-class career Neale scored 17,445 runs (av 36.49). After his playing career, he became the England team's operations manager.

Phil Neale on New Road:
"We clinched several of our trophies with big victories in front of packed houses at New Road and we were able fully to share our success with the loyal supporters – the Championship win in 1988, the win over Glamorgan to retain the title in 1989 after the wicket had been vandalised, and two Sunday League triumphs in 1987 and 1988 when the titles were secured with comprehensive 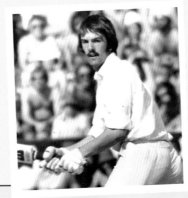 *home victories. The bond with New Road and our supporters was such that, after our first Lord's victory in the Benson & Hedges Cup in 1991, we even travelled back to the ground to celebrate on home turf with our supporters and families."*

Vikram Solanki

Born in India in 1976, Vikram Solanki made his limited-overs debut for the county aged just 17 and has been the Worcestershire captain since 2005. A graceful batsman, Solanki has played more than 50 one-day internationals for England, with two centuries, but has not been given the chance to play Test cricket. In 2008 he led Worcestershire back to Division One of the County Championship and made his highest score – 270 against Gloucestershire.

Vikram Solanki on New Road:
"The New Road ground is the esssence of county cricket; you can't compare it to any other sporting venues in the country. It is an idyllic setting for first-class cricket and I am lucky enough to have been with the club since I was a 15-year-old. To walk out onto the field in front of your home crowd is incomparable, especially as Worcestershire have great members and fans who always give a warm friendly reception and long may that continue."

Henry Olonga

Henry Olonga (born 1976) made his debut for Zimbabwe at the age of 18, the youngest man to play for that country. The fact that he was also the first black cricketer ever to represent Zimbabwe added to the impact of the brave protest which he and Andy Flower made at the 2003 World Cup in wearing black armbands "mourning the death of democracy in our beloved Zimbabwe". As a result, a warrant was issued for his arrest on charges of treason and Olonga was forced to retire from international cricket and, for a short time, to go into hiding. As an extremely fast, if sometimes inaccurate, bowler, Olonga had played 30 Tests, taking 68 wickets, and 50 one-day internationals, with best figures of 6-19 against England in 2000. He is now a cricket commentator and singer.

Henry Olonga on New Road:
"My fondest memory of a cricket ground happens to be of New Road. Zimbabwe played a match against Sri Lanka there in the 1999 World Cup and it is of particular fondness for me not because I had an especially good day there – but because it is one of the prettiest grounds I have ever seen. For me what makes the ground so unique is the feeling that it hasn't quite graduated from being a little village venue compared to some of the concrete behemoths that exist in other parts of the country. Of course, the cherry on the cake is the cathedral as the backdrop to this magnificent landscape. Quintessentially English."

YORKSHIRE

Yorkshire are justifiably proud of their cricketing heritage and achievements, and their unparalleled record of 31 Championship crowns. Cricket in the county was originally centred on Sheffield, and it was there that the team became known as Yorkshire in 1833.

A local side played against a Manchester team in 1849, in a fixture described as Yorkshire versus Lancashire. This is commonly regarded as the first unofficial Roses Match, although the first official contest took place in 1867. Yorkshire CCC was officially formed in 1863, at a meeting at a hotel in Sheffield. The county developed into a formidable side, first becoming Champion County in 1867 and winning the title regularly in the decades that followed. Further success followed after their move from Sheffield to Leeds, completed in 1891.

Lord Hawke, who had taken over the captaincy in 1883, was a dominant figure at the club and remained the leader on the field for 28 very successful seasons. Hawke steered the county to three Championships in the 1890s and three more in consecutive seasons from 1900 to 1902, when the all-conquering side lost only two matches out of a total of 60. Three further Championships followed between 1903 and 1914, when significant contributions were made with both bat and ball by George Hirst – who in 1906 performed the unique feat of scoring over 2,000 runs and taking over 200 wickets – and Wilfred Rhodes, who in both 1909 and 1911 scored more than 2,000 runs and took over 100 wickets.

Yorkshire were the dominant force in English cricket during the inter-War years; for instance in four Championship-winning seasons from 1922 to 1925 they lost only six matches out of 122. At this time the mainstays of the batting were the openers, Percy

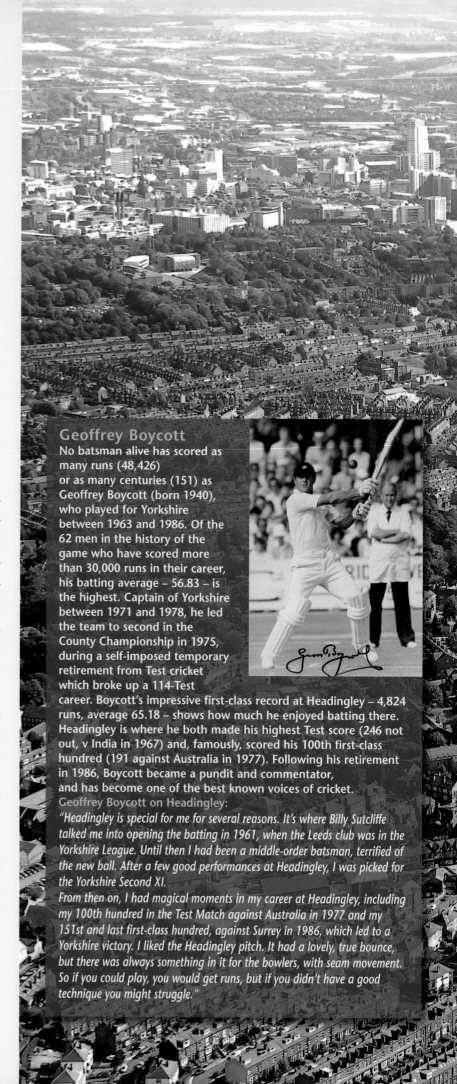

Geoffrey Boycott

No batsman alive has scored as many runs (48,426) or as many centuries (151) as Geoffrey Boycott (born 1940), who played for Yorkshire between 1963 and 1986. Of the 62 men in the history of the game who have scored more than 30,000 runs in their career, his batting average – 56.83 – is the highest. Captain of Yorkshire between 1971 and 1978, he led the team to second in the County Championship in 1975, during a self-imposed temporary retirement from Test cricket which broke up a 114-Test career. Boycott's impressive first-class record at Headingley – 4,824 runs, average 65.18 – shows how much he enjoyed batting there. Headingley is where he both made his highest Test score (246 not out, v India in 1967) and, famously, scored his 100th first-class hundred (191 against Australia in 1977). Following his retirement in 1986, Boycott became a pundit and commentator, and has become one of the best known voices of cricket.

Geoffrey Boycott on Headingley:

"Headingley is special for me for several reasons. It's where Billy Sutcliffe talked me into opening the batting in 1961, when the Leeds club was in the Yorkshire League. Until then I had been a middle-order batsman, terrified of the new ball. After a few good performances at Headingley, I was picked for the Yorkshire Second XI.

From then on, I had magical moments in my career at Headingley, including my 100th hundred in the Test Match against Australia in 1977 and my 151st and last first-class hundred, against Surrey in 1986, which led to a Yorkshire victory. I liked the Headingley pitch. It had a lovely, true bounce, but there was always something in it for the bowlers, with seam movement. So if you could play, you would get runs, but if you didn't have a good technique you might struggle."

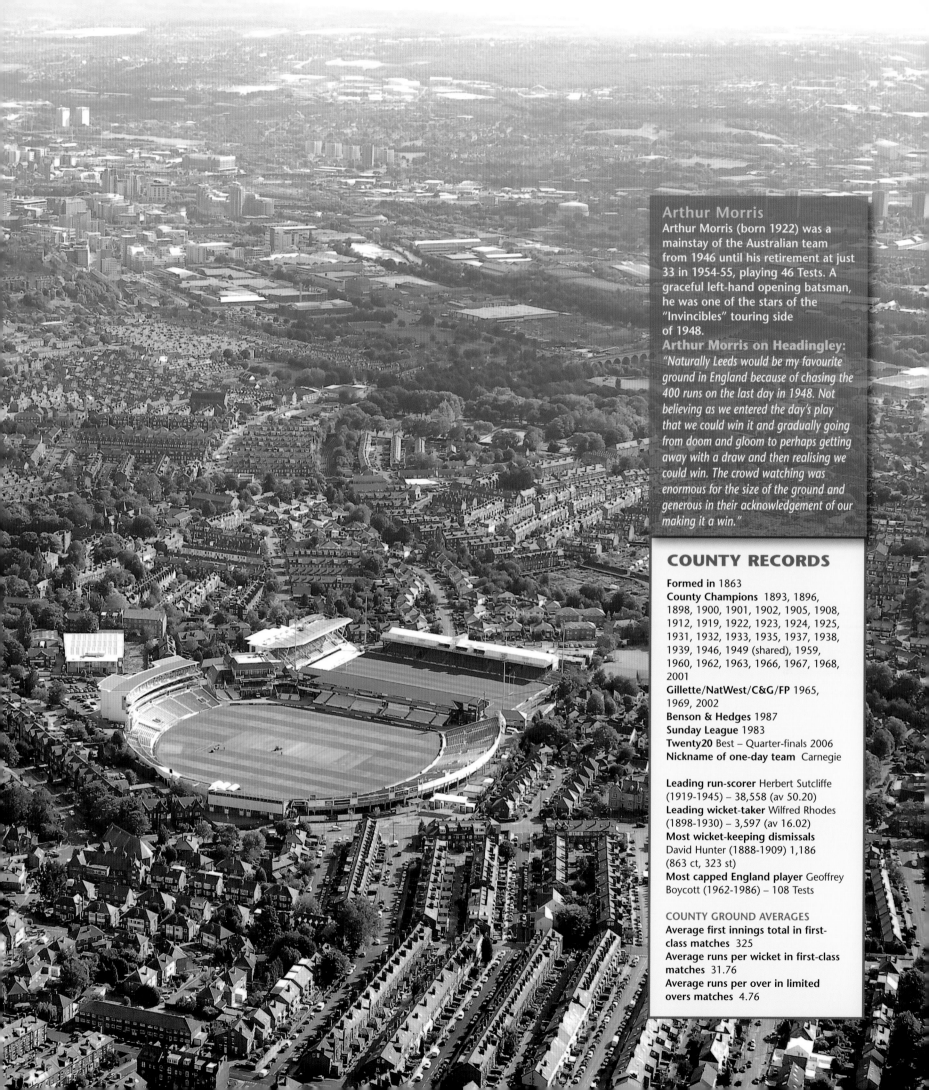

Arthur Morris

Arthur Morris (born 1922) was a mainstay of the Australian team from 1946 until his retirement at just 33 in 1954-55, playing 46 Tests. A graceful left-hand opening batsman, he was one of the stars of the "Invincibles" touring side of 1948.

Arthur Morris on Headingley:
"Naturally Leeds would be my favourite ground in England because of chasing the 400 runs on the last day in 1948. Not believing as we entered the day's play that we could win it and gradually going from doom and gloom to perhaps getting away with a draw and then realising we could win. The crowd watching was enormous for the size of the ground and generous in their acknowledgement of our making it a win."

COUNTY RECORDS

Formed in 1863
County Champions 1893, 1896, 1898, 1900, 1901, 1902, 1905, 1908, 1912, 1919, 1922, 1923, 1924, 1925, 1931, 1932, 1933, 1935, 1937, 1938, 1939, 1946, 1949 (shared), 1959, 1960, 1962, 1963, 1966, 1967, 1968, 2001
Gillette/NatWest/C&G/FP 1965, 1969, 2002
Benson & Hedges 1987
Sunday League 1983
Twenty20 Best – Quarter-finals 2006
Nickname of one-day team Carnegie

Leading run-scorer Herbert Sutcliffe (1919-1945) – 38,558 (av 50.20)
Leading wicket-taker Wilfred Rhodes (1898-1930) – 3,597 (av 16.02)
Most wicket-keeping dismissals David Hunter (1888-1909) 1,186 (863 ct, 323 st)
Most capped England player Geoffrey Boycott (1962-1986) – 108 Tests

COUNTY GROUND AVERAGES
Average first innings total in first-class matches 325
Average runs per wicket in first-class matches 31.76
Average runs per over in limited overs matches 4.76

Holmes and Herbert Sutcliffe, who shared 69 century opening stands, 18 of them in excess of 250, and in 1932 famously put on 555 for the first wicket against Essex at Leyton in just 7 hours and 25 minutes.

In the 1930s Yorkshire won seven Championships in nine seasons, and England caps were awarded to 12 Yorkshire players. The prolific Maurice Leyland made nine centuries for England, whilst left-arm spinner Hedley Verity took almost 2,000 wickets, including the best innings figures ever, 10-10 against Nottinghamshire in 1932. That decade also saw the emergence of Len Hutton, who made his debut at county level in 1934 and, by the time of his retirement in 1955, had scored 24,807 runs and 85 centuries for Yorkshire. Among his triumphs as a batsman – and as a shrewd captain who regained the Ashes in 1953 and retained them in Australia in 1954-55 – Hutton is particularly remembered for the 364 he made for England against Australia at The Oval in 1938, which remains the highest innings by an Englishman in Test Matches.

In the 1950s, five second-place finishes in Surrey's remarkable decade were scant consolation for supporters who had grown accustomed to continual success, but a Championship was won in 1959 and six more followed over the next decade, latterly under the leadership of Brian Close, who took over the captaincy from Vic Wilson in 1962. In this era, the bowling was led by Fred Trueman; other key players were Geoffrey Boycott and all-rounder Ray Illingworth. After 1968, however, Yorkshire had to wait 33 years for their next Championship, under the leadership of David Byas. Overall Yorkshire have won the Championship 30 times outright, and shared it on one occasion. It was not until 1958 that the county slipped below 10th in the table and in 1983 the unthinkable happened when Yorkshire finished bottom of the table for the first time. It was little consolation in that latter year for the county to win the Sunday League.

The county has produced some of the legends of English cricket from batsmen Sutcliffe, Hutton and Boycott to bowlers Trueman, Rhodes, Verity and Darren Gough. This flow of talent fuelled the idea that a strong Yorkshire meant a strong England team. Yorkshire's past achievements and cricketing tradition make it a county always worth watching out for.

Headingley Carnegie, Leeds

Situated in the heart of Leeds, Headingley is the home not only of Yorkshire cricket, but also of local rugby teams, from both Union and League. As a major sporting venue, it has hosted

international fixtures in both cricket and rugby. Although Yorkshire cricket was initially based at Bramall Lane, Sheffield, it was not long before it moved its base to Leeds. This was triggered by the purchase of the land in 1888 by a group of businessmen who established the Leeds Cricket, Football and Athletic Company. They had an interest in developing local sport, and rugby and cricket were first played on the ground in 1890. Yorkshire's first county match took place the following year and

Imran Khan

Now a well-known public figure and Pakistani politician, Imran Khan (born 1952) was one of the most talented and effective all-rounders of his generation. A talismanic figure and inspirational captain, he led Pakistan for almost a decade. In all, he played 88 Tests, averaging 37.69 with the bat (3,807 runs) and 22.81 with the ball (capturing 362 wickets), as well as 175 one-day international matches. After playing for Oxford University between 1973 and 1975, captaining the university in 1975, he went on to play county cricket for Worcestershire and Sussex. In 1987 he led Pakistan to its first-ever series victory over England in England, bowling his team to victory at Headingley in the third Test, with match figures of 10-77. There was a fitting end to Imran's international career, as he bowed out by leading Pakistan to victory in the 1992 World Cup in Australia. After retiring from cricket, Imran became a charity worker and a politician in Pakistan. He is the Chairman of the Pakistan tehreek-e-insaaf (Movement for Justice) party, which he founded in 1996, whose aim is to empower the people of Pakistan by promoting justice, humanity and self-esteem through policies which include establishing a welfare state and an independent judiciary (www.ptiuk.org).

Imran Khan on Headingley:

"From the outset my ambition was to play Test cricket, and the ground on which I particularly enjoyed playing Test Matches was Headingley. It was a sporting wicket. Batting was a challenge, and conditions were usually good for bowling, as the ball would swing. I liked bowling there as the ball used to move about a bit, although if it was sunny you had to use skill to bowl the batsman out. I loved the atmosphere created by the crowd, which was always very knowledgeable and appreciated the finer points of the game. A lot of them seemed to be club cricketers. Whilst every game I played at Headingley from my first Test there in 1974 was interesting, I recall with particular pride our win there in 1987, as a result of which Pakistan won its first series victory in England."

the ground's stature was confirmed by the staging of its first Test Match, England v Australia, in 1899. Thereafter, Headingley became the official headquarters of Yorkshire cricket.

Whilst the pavilion at the ground dates from its construction in 1898/99, the ground developed in the early decades of the 20th century, enhancing its infrastructure to become a major cricketing venue. A local building contractor, Sir Edward Airey, was commissioned to carry out redevelopments in 1932 and the

Main Stand was completed soon after – replacing the Rugby Stand which had been destroyed in a fire at a rugby match.

The ground has benefited from major refurbishment in recent years. In the 1990s a campaign for the county to move to a new greenfield site in Wakefield was successfully resisted. The redeveloped Western Terrace, costing £32m and with seating for 7,500 spectators, was opened in 2001. The following year, the newly built East Stand, with three tiers and seating for 1,700

HEADINGLEY CARNEGIE, LEEDS

Address Headingley Carnegie
Cricket Ground
Leeds LS6 3BU
Main tel 0871 971 1222
Website www.yorkshireccc.com

Ends Football Stand End, Kirkstall Lane End
Capacity 17,000
First County Match Yorkshire v Kent
(24 August 1891)
First Test Match England v Australia
(29 June 1899)
First ODI England v West Indies (5 September 1973)
Record crowd 44,507 Yorkshire v Lancashire
(15 May 1948)

Scoreboard

Main
Stand

Football
Stand End

Kirkstall
Lane End

KIRKSTALL LANE

ST MICHAEL'S LANE

Scoreboard

members, was opened. Various parts of the ground are named after famous Yorkshire cricketers, from the Sir Leonard Hutton Gates to the "Dickie" Bird Clock.

In December 2005 Yorkshire CCC bought the ground for £12m, and it was subsequently renamed the Headingley Carnegie Stadium. The club has planning permission for major redevelopments, which should be completed by the start of the 2010 season. The focal point will be a new five-storey pavilion, the Carnegie Pavilion, to be built at a cost of £14 million, which will also serve as a teaching facility for Leeds Metropolitan University.

Headingley has hosted some memorable Test Matches, most notably when England staged a heroic comeback to beat Australia in 1981. This match was only the second time ever that a side following-on in a Test Match had won, and the comeback, inspired by Ian Botham's famous 149 not out and Bob Willis' furious fast bowling which yielded figures of 8-43, is still regarded as one of the greatest of all time.

FAMOUS PLAYERS

Lord Hawke

Although born in Lincolnshire, Lord Hawke (1860-1938) managed to avoid the then requirement for Yorkshire players to have been born in the county, and made his debut for Yorkshire in 1881. Two years later, when still a Cambridge undergraduate, he became Yorkshire captain, a position he was to occupy for 28 years. Further consolidating his control of the county, he was President of Yorkshire from 1898 until his death, and was instrumental in its move from Bramall Lane to Headingley. His long period as a captain who behaved as a benevolent dictator brought great success, including eight

Championships. Noted for his off-side hitting, Hawke scored 16,749 runs (av 20.19) in 633 first-class matches. When making his highest score, 166, in Yorkshire's 887 against Warwickshire in 1896 – the highest innings total in county cricket – he shared a partnership of 292 with Robert Peel which remains the highest eighth wicket partnership in English first-class cricket. However, in his five Tests, Hawke met with little success, scoring only 55 runs from seven completed innings. Lord Hawke was an ambassador for cricket, a game he loved dearly, once writing "cricket is a moral lesson in itself".

Ray Illingworth

A gritty player and uncompromising character, Ray Illingworth (born 1932) was a spin bowler and doughty batsman who was blessed with a shrewd cricketing brain. Born in Pudsey, he made his debut for Yorkshire in 1951, was capped in 1955 and enjoyed considerable success for the county until, following a contractual dispute at the end of the 1968 season, he left to captain Leicestershire. He led the Midlands county to the Benson and Hedges Cup in 1972 (ironically beating Yorkshire in the final) and to its first-ever Championship in 1975. In 1969, following an injury to Colin Cowdrey, he became England captain. A great success in that role, he brought out the best in his charges – especially the fast bowler John Snow – and was renowned for his astute field placings. He regained the Ashes in Australia in 1970-71 and retained them in England in 1972. His record as England captain was impressive: 12 won, 14 drawn and just 5 lost.

His England career encompassed 61 Tests between 1958 and 1973, in which he took 122 wickets and scored 1,836 runs. On retiring from first-class cricket in 1978, he became Yorkshire team manager – although he returned to play as captain, aged 50, in 1982, and then carved out a career as a media pundit before becoming England coach and Chairman of Selectors in 1997.

Ray Illingworth on Bradford:
"My favourite cricket ground is Bradford Park Avenue. I played there for almost 40 years, the first time for Farsley in the Priestley Cup Final in 1949, when I was 17. After retiring from first-class cricket I went back to playing for Farsley in the Bradford League until I was 55 years old. I first played at Bradford for Yorkshire in 1953, and it was there that I received my Yorkshire cap from Norman Yardley in 1955. Being capped by Yorkshire meant more to me than anything else at that time – I only dreamt of getting a Yorkshire cap. As the Gloucestershire and England spinner John Mortimore once put it, Bradford was the only ground in England where you put a side into bat on a green pitch and then found yourself being bowled out by spinners at the end of the first day. We always got exciting cricket at Bradford. You didn't need to manufacture a finish – people had to be bowled out, there were no declarations. We played on uncovered wickets, and if it rained the crowd would stream in – they knew it would be interesting cricket.

Bradford was also the best ground in the world for watching cricket. It was a bullring – the ground was wide but not straight – and was the best I've ever played on for viewing. The crowd created a wonderful atmosphere – but an intimidating one for the opposition."

Rachael Heyhoe-Flint

One of the best-known women cricketers to have played the game at the highest level, Rachael Hayhoe-Flint's Test career spanned from 1960 to 1979. Born in 1939, she became captain in 1966 and led England to a World Cup victory in 1973, continuing as captain until 1977. By the time she played her last Test in 1979, her 1,594 runs in 22 Tests established a world-record at the time. Such was her stature as a run-scorer that she returned briefly to the England side for the 1982 World Cup, at the age of 43.

She has maintained a high profile as an ambassador for women's cricket and became one of the first female members of the MCC. Though best known for her cricket, she also represented England at hockey, as a goalkeeper. She boasts a batting average of 69 at Scarborough.

Darren Gough

A swashbuckling fast bowler, born in Barnsley in 1970, Darren Gough is a Yorkshire lad through and through. After making his debut aged just 18 in 1989, he served Yorkshire for 15 years before joining Essex in 2004 for three years; he then returned to his native county as captain in 2007 for the final two seasons of his career. For England, he was an entertaining and highly successful performer. The powerfully-built Yorkshireman became England's main strike bowler, using a range of weaponry including reverse swing, slower balls and yorkers. A particular highlight was the hat-trick he took against Australia at Sydney in January 1999. Fittingly, it was at Headingley that in 1998 Gough helped England to a 2-1 series victory over South Africa with his best Test figures of 6-42. By the end of his Test career in 2003, he had taken 229 wickets (at a very

respectable average of 28.39) in 58 Tests (he would have played more but for a series of injuries) and contributed some useful runs, without ever turning into the genuine all-rounder that his early form promised. He continued to play one-day internationals and finished with an English record 234 wickets in this format from 158 games. A flamboyant performer, Gough has developed his career outside the game, as a media personality and by winning the BBC ballroom dancing series *Strictly Come Dancing* in 2005.

Darren Gough on Headingley:
"I've had some wonderful games and Test Matches at Headingley. I've done well with both bat and ball and really enjoyed it. I'm glad I'm retiring as it is getting flatter and flatter and it is due for a resurface. When I was wearing England colours and playing in front of my home crowd it was brilliant. One memory I have was when we beat South Africa and I got the last wicket. It was a great atmosphere as it always is at Headingley – the Western Terrace gets a lot of stick, but is one of the greatest crowds to play in front of."

OTHER GROUNDS

North Marine Road Ground, Scarborough *above*

The North Marine Road Ground, Scarborough has a capacity of 11,500. Yorkshire first played there in 1874, and it remains a tradition to this day for the county to play there during the Scarborough Festival. Scarborough Cricket Club leased the ground for £15 a year until 1878, when it purchased the ground. In 1895, a pavilion was built, and stands were added in 1926, and most recently the West Stand in 1956. The ground has hosted international cricket: England played two one-day games there, against the West Indies in 1976 and against New Zealand in 1978.

Rachael Heyhoe-Flint on Scarborough:

"Scarborough cricket ground has always held special memories for me. In 1963 I played my first home Test series against Australia as a 'promising youngster'. The Second Test at Scarborough was the first time I ever experienced 'sea-fret stops play!' This was not because the players were in difficulty, but because the scorers, high above us, couldn't work out, through the gathering fret, what we were up to at sea level, so to speak!

My second appearance at the seaside venue was in a Test in June 1966 – my debut as England captain! No fog this time, but glorious sunshine. I was aware that there was some opposition to my appointment as captain – a local paper described me as 'a controversial character' – so I felt I had to prove myself (a bit like Kevin Pietersen, but without the reverse sweep!)

Batting first, I came in at number three, 20 minutes before lunch. I was 97 not out at tea. Two singles and a cover-drive for two brought up my century – and I still hold that memory very highly in my cricket career thanks, of course, to a great batting track at Scarborough!

Next day I bought all the Sunday papers to read about my century – being a shy, modest introvert! Not a mention in any except The Sunday Telegraph – a tiny line score underneath the bowls column! I made a pledge there and then to market and promote women's cricket because we got such scant recognition. I am still trying more than 40 years later!"

Bramall Lane, Sheffield (*not pictured*)

Originally the headquarters of Yorkshire cricket before the move to Headingley, it is now more famous for being the home of the football team, Sheffield United. It hosted its only ever Test Match in 1902, when Australia defeated England by 143 runs, and was closed as a cricket venue in 1973.

St George's Road Ground, Harrogate *below*

The St George's Road Ground was established in 1877, and the main pavilion dates from 1896. It first hosted a first-class match in 1882 and Yorkshire first played there in 1894 in a match against Leicestershire. The ground benefited from the construction of the Mound in 1956 and the Tavern bar in 1965. The county played there sporadically but since 1974 Harrogate has been established as a festival ground, with Yorkshire traditionally playing there once a season. In 1996 a charity match between India and Pakistan attracted a record 15,000 spectators to the ground.

In August 2010, St George's Road is due to host the 14th World Cricket Festival – a tournament for "Golden Oldies" (whose members must be over 40 years of age) which includes teams from around the world.

OXFORD UNIVERSITY

As its name suggests, The Parks is located in the middle of the University Parks, a few minutes' walk from Oxford city centre. The cricket ground occupies 10 of the Parks' 74 acres. Since it is not separated from the remainder of the public park – the only permanent structure is the oft-photographed and evocative pavilion, which was built in 1881 and was designed by Sir Thomas Jackson, the architect of the university's Examination Schools – admission fees cannot be charged for casual spectators who do not sit on the benches dotted around the ground. (Entrance to the pavilion is limited to players, members of the OUCC and the press.) Cricket is not played on The Parks after the university summer term; in August and September grass court tennis is played on the outfield in the shadow of the pavilion.

Although cricket in Oxford was first mentioned in 1727, and a survey and plan for two cricket grounds at The Parks were prepared in 1867, it was only in 1881 that cricket was first played at The Parks. The instigator of this development was Dr Evans, the Master of Pembroke College, who managed to persuade the university to grant a lease of the land. Three years later, Oxford defeated the touring Australians by seven wickets. In 1886 WG Grace, playing for the MCC, scored 104 and then took all 10 Oxford wickets for 49 runs – the only time any bowler has taken 10 wickets in an innings at The Parks. The highest score made at The Parks is 266 not out by Lancashire opening bat Winston Place in 1947; the best stand, the 395 with which Martin Young and Ronald Nicholls opened the Gloucestershire innings in 1962.

The Parks

Address University Parks, Parks Road, Oxford OX1 3RF
Main tel 01865 557106 or 07899 846878
Website www.cricketintheparks.org.uk
Formed in 1827
First first-class match
Oxford University v MCC
(16 May 1881)
Ends Pavilion End, Norham Gardens End

GROUND AVERAGES
Average first innings total in first-class matches 329
Average runs per wicket in first-class matches 35.92

George Chesterton
George Chesterton (born 1922) played for Oxford in 1949, and subsequently for Worcestershire and MCC. He later co-authored, with Hubert Doggart, *Oxford and Cambridge Cricket.*
George Chesterton on The Parks:
"1947 was my first summer at Oxford, a glorious time, the sun always seemed to be shining. I played cricket almost every day sampling nearly all the superb college grounds. Yet whenever I found time The Parks beckoned. It has a true parkland quality with the beautiful ground surrounded by trees of magnificent stature, including at that time a line of splendid elms. Tucked amongst the trees is the unchanged Victorian pavilion, built with the intention that the wicket should be the same distance from the pavilion as it is at Lord's. The great attraction in this glorious summer was the New Zealand batsman Martin Donnelly. The word used to get around that he was at the wicket and the lecture halls would empty and within only minutes, it seemed, there were enthusiasts four deep behind the ropes at this spectacular free entertainment."

Alan Smith
Alan Smith (born 1936) was an Oxford blue between 1958 and 1960, captaining the side, and later captained Warwickshire. A wicket-keeper batsman, he made 776 dismissals in his career (715 ct, 61 st) and played six Tests for England, against Australia and New Zealand in 1962-63.
Alan Smith on The Parks:
"The Parks is a beautiful and atmospheric place in which to begin one's career. In 1958 there was a full programme of county matches and big names – including Trueman, Graveney and Washbrook – appeared in my first fortnight. I felt honoured to be following in the footsteps of the many distinguished names on the honours boards. These dated back to 1827, and included CB Fry, 'Plum' Warner and Douglas Jardine. I was fortunate to play in a brief 'golden era'. My team-mates were talented cricketers, some from the sub-continent, and good enough to achieve quite a few victories against full-strength counties."

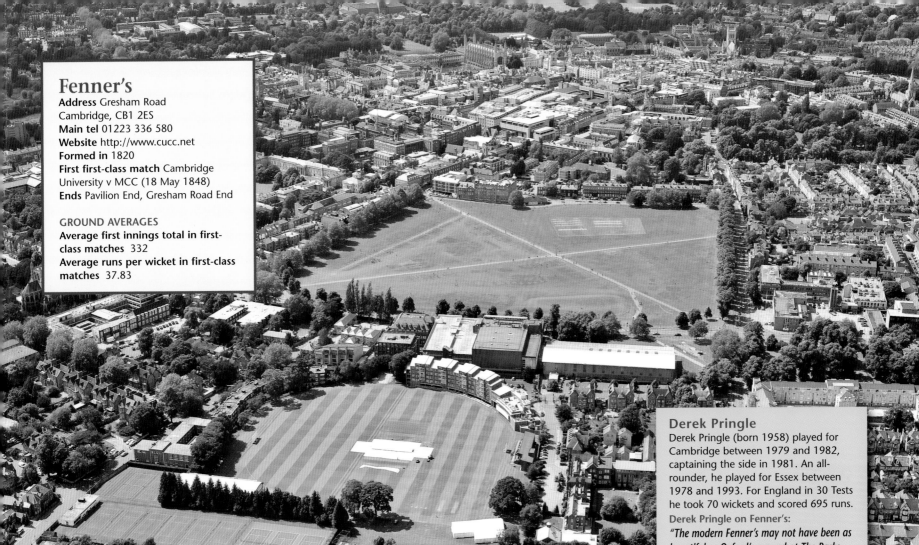

CAMBRIDGE UNIVERSITY

Fenner's has been the home of Cambridge University Cricket Club since 1848, when Mr F P Fenner leased the land from Gonville and Caius College. The University Cricket Club had been established in 1820 and the first match against Oxford took place in June, 1827 at Lord's, although there is evidence of students first playing a cricket match in 1755 against the Gentlemen of Eton. The freehold of the ground was bought in 1894 and in 1976 the university became fully responsible for Fenner's in place of a trust. There are no permanent stands at Fenner's and the pavilion, previously wooden, was rebuilt in 1972.

Fenner's has hosted some of the stars of world cricket, but they have not always necessarily shone at Fenner's. Sir Donald Bradman was bowled for a duck by Cambridge's Jack Davies in 1934. However, Sir Everton Weekes and the touring West Indians of 1950 fared a lot better. Weekes' 304 not out remains the highest ever score at the ground, as is the West Indians' total of 730-3. This was in response to the students' 594 for 4 declared. The match was an extraordinary run feast still talked about today.

As well as serving as the home of the university team, Fenner's is home to a number of other cricket matches, including schools and women's cricket. Since 2000 Cambridge has been an ECB Centre of Cricketing Excellence and the Cambridge squad includes players from the university and Anglia Ruskin University.

Derek Pringle
Derek Pringle (born 1958) played for Cambridge between 1979 and 1982, captaining the side in 1981. An all-rounder, he played for Essex between 1978 and 1993. For England in 30 Tests he took 70 wickets and scored 695 runs.
Derek Pringle on Fenner's:
"The modern Fenner's may not have been as beautiful as Oxford's ground at The Parks, but it was a better place to learn cricket. The pitch there, lovingly nurtured for decades by local legend Cyril Coote, was a batsman's paradise and therefore tested a bowler's range and mettle to the hilt. Heartache often ensued but if you could get wickets at Fenner's you could get them anywhere. Favourite memories include playing the West Indies there in 1980, a match in which we competed favourably until about tea on the first day, when our skipper inexplicably declared, and our victory over Lancashire in 1982, which was watched by a goodly crowd of about 2,000. Being beaten by a university team, no great rarity before the 1960s, was unheard of by that stage, though our pride only turned to deep satisfaction once we discovered that Lancashire's committee had held an inquiry afterwards."

Dennis Silk (see page 128) on Fenner's:
"Fenner's will always be a sacred ground for me, not that I made many runs there, but much more because of the friendships I made on and off the field. To play first-class cricket as an undergraduate with men of the stature of Len Hutton, Peter May, Fred Trueman and Keith Miller was an excitement in itself, but to get to know professional cricketers as a whole, who were our heroes, was to realise why cricket is such a wonderful game."

Lord Griffiths

Lord Griffiths (born 1923) played for Cambridge between 1946 and 1948, taking 5-84 in the first innings of the 1946 Varsity match. A fast bowler, he also played as an amateur for Glamorgan, including in 1948 when it won the Championship. He ended up with 102 first-class wickets. In 1985 he became a Law Lord. A keen golfer, he was Captain of the Royal and Ancient Golf Club of St Andrews in 1993, the only man to hold that post and the presidency of the MCC. During the Second World War, Lord Griffiths was awarded the Military Cross for his bravery in disarming a tank.

Lord Griffiths on Fenner's:

"I had the good fortune to play at Fenner's in the Cambridge University cricket side through the summers of 1946, '47 and '48. In situation and size it is the ideal university ground, tucked away from the noise of traffic, yet close to the centre of the town and the colleges and not too large. The groundsman in my day, Cyril Coote,

kept it in immaculate condition. Not a weed was to be seen on the turf. He kept a passive wicket on the square, which was sensible as young university batsmen encountering county cricket for the first time would have been in serious trouble against county bowlers on lively wickets. But it was heartbreaking to bowl on, the ball hardly ever rose above stump height, nor did it seam much or take

spin. However, I suppose it taught us to bowl line and length and we had our reward when we went on tour to the county grounds, whose wickets were very different.

When the great 1948 Australian side visited Fenner's, after the first day's play the teams dined together in my college, St John's, and then adjourned to continue the evening in my rooms in college. Neil Harvey and Lindsay Hassett goaded me and somewhere near midnight Hassett was playing chip shots over my sofa into a wastepaper basket, when I, flush with drink, said: "Hassett, you haven't got a fast bowler that could knock the skin off a rice pudding". Now this was a serious error because although Bradman had not come to Fenner's both Lindwall and Miller were playing.

When next day I went in to bat at number 10, Hassett called for the ball, tossed it to Lindwall and said: "Ray, just condition the lad a bit." I have never been more terrified in my life. Remember in those days we had no helmets, armguards, body belts or thigh pads, just pads and a box. "Don't flinch, Griffiths, don't flinch" I kept repeating to myself and as Lindwall came to his delivery stride I took a step forward to meet him. I never saw the ball after it pitched and there followed

either a sickening thud as it hit Tallon's gloves standing some twenty yards back or a piercing pain in some part of my body. I survived the over owing to a hitherto unsuspected streak of sadism in our umpire George Watts, who refused to give me out lbw.

Worse was to come: the ball was now given to Keith Miller, who struck my box such a blow that no amount of hammering with a bat handle has ever been able to remove the dent. How thankful I am that boxes in those days were vast codpieces of steel and leather bound on with straps – and not the little pieces of plastic they now slip into their jockstraps! I only lasted about four overs, but I treasure the experience of facing one of the quickest pairs of opening bowlers the game has known."

GHG Doggart

Hubert Doggart (born 1925) was a talented all-round sportsman, who was awarded a Cambridge Blue in five different sports (cricket, football, squash, racquets and fives) and was captain of four university teams. A graceful middle-order batsman, Doggart made 215 not out on his first-class debut, against Lancashire at Fenner's in 1948. The following year, he made an unbeaten 219 against Essex, sharing an unbroken partnership of 429 with John Dewes which remains the highest stand for any wicket both for Cambridge and at Fenner's. In 1950, as an undergraduate, he played two Tests. Doggart scored 1,750 runs at Fenner's (av 58.33). He played for Sussex periodically until 1961, captaining the side in 1954. He was later headmaster of King's School, Bruton.

Hubert Doggart on Fenner's:

"My memory starts with a personal reminiscence, the first match of the 1948 season against a strong Lancashire side when on debut I carved a niche in Wisden's records. I recall, too, the match against Essex in 1949 when John Dewes and I had an unbroken partnership of 429. The match started twenty minutes late, and Doug Insole, our captain, was going to declare at 5.50 pm or thereabouts but was persuaded to allow us to go on to attempt to pass the then world record second wicket stand of 455. We were not told, however, or else we could have had a dart at the record that evening. As it turned out, Doug rightly declared on Monday morning and tens of reporters and photographers went away empty-handed. Essex had their full attack out so it was a great pleasure to play so well and set up the then English record.

Another memory is of the tourist match with the West Indies in 1950, when we made 507 for 3 on the first day, David Sheppard and John Dewes putting on 343 for the first wicket with an excellent display of stroke-play (they did it again later that season at Hove against Sussex, with an opening stand of 349). I chose to bat on on the second day to give Peter May a chance to play an innings: it was a mistake as the West Indies batted for the rest of the match, making

730 for 3. Frank Worrell scored 160 and Everton Weekes 304 not out. Everton was heard, in the 290s, muttering to himself: "Play carefully, Weekes man, in the nineties"!

I used to enjoy the old Victorian pavilion, which had more character than its successor built at the other end of the ground. There was much "laughter and the love of friends" within. As after the First World War, undergraduates were older and more experienced and this was reflected in the cricket played."

Dennis Silk

Born in California in 1931, Dennis Silk played for Cambridge between 1953 and 1955, twice scoring a century in the Varsity match. Silk went on to play for Somerset and the MCC. He was Warden of Radley College between 1968 and 1991.

The Rev Andrew Wingfield Digby

(born 1950) was a theology student when he played for Oxford between 1971 and 1977, winning four Blues. A medium-paced bowler, he played 39 first class matches, taking 96 wickets (av 33.87). The first full-time employee of Christians in Sport, he was chaplain at the 1988 Seoul Olympics and in 1989 was appointed by Ted Dexter, the then chairman of selectors, as spiritual advisor to the England cricket team. Since 2002 Wingfield Digby has been vicar of St Andrew's Church, Oxford. In 2008 he captained Oxfordshire to a three-run victory in the final of the 50+ County Championship at Lord's.

The Rev Andrew Wingfield Digby on The Parks:

"The old pavilion has a timeless air to it. This is in part due to the traditional style, the white facing and railings, the old clock, which I saw Mike Procter put a ball straight through, but mainly because it is situated right in the middle of a park – as old cricket pitches used to be... only Arundel can compare, really.

Inside on the long room walls are the names of every "Blues" team – you'll even find me if you look hard in the top right hand corner, amidst the Frys, Cowdreys, Pataudis and Khans etc. Outside it's the trees you'll notice first – a glorious arboreal backdrop to every game. And finally the memories – Viv Richards playing for Somerset and edging my first ball to him to the keeper. IVA Richards c Fisher b Wingfield Digby 5. 'You stick to preaching, Man', said the great one years later – he had not forgotten.

And numerous magical days in the spring, girls in diaphanous dresses strolling the boundary, world-class players knocking us to kingdom come. It couldn't last for ever, but it should."